D0143241

Doing Qualitative Research Differently

Doing Qualitative Research Differently

free association, narrative and the interview method

Wendy Hollway and Tony Jefferson

WITHDRAWN

PROPERTY OF
SENECA COLLEGE
LEARNING COMMONS
NEWNHAM CAMPUS

SAGE Publications

London • Thousand Oaks • New Delhi

© Wendy Hollway and Tony Jefferson 2000

First published 2000. Reprinted 2001, 2002

All rights reserved. No part of this publication may be
reproduced, stored in a retrieval system, transmitted or
utilized in any form or by any means, electronic, mechanical,
photocopying, recording or otherwise, without permission in
writing from the Publishers.

 SAGE Publications Ltd
6 Bonhill Street
London EC2A 4PU

SAGE Publications Inc.
2455 Teller Road
Thousand Oaks, California 91320

SAGE Publications India Pvt Ltd
32, M-Block Market
Greater Kailash - I
New Delhi 110 048

British Library Cataloguing in Publication data

A catalogue record for this book is available from
the British Library

ISBN 0 7619 6425 8
ISBN 0 7619 6426 6 (pbk)

Library of Congress catalog card record available

Typeset by SIVA Math Setters, Chennai, India.
Printed in Great Britain by The Cromwell Press Ltd
Trowbridge, Wiltshire

CONTENTS

ACKNOWLEDGEMENTS

This book results from our Economic and Social Research Council (ESRC) project on 'Gender difference, anxiety and the fear of crime' (no. L210252018), which was part of the ESRC Crime and Social Order Programme, directed by Tim Hope. We thank the ESRC for its financial support, especially its willingness to invest in theoretically driven projects, and Tim for arranging a variety of stimulating get-togethers with the other project grant-holders. We are also grateful to Robin Humphrey, who organised the biographical-interpretative methods workshop, led by Roswitha Breckner and Bettina Volter. There we first encountered the approach which we went on to adapt and develop into the free-association narrative interview method. The statistics department of a local police force was helpful in identifying our high- and low-crime locations. Stephen Frosh, our consultant, and Michael Rustin were always helpful and supportive. Dawn Lessels reliably and efficiently managed the painstaking work of transcribing over 80 audiotaped interviews. Prue Chamberlayne and the Biography in Social Policy Unit at the University of East London provided an encouraging forum for testing out some of our ideas. Special thanks are due to those who read and commented so constructively on our draft manuscript, namely, Lynn Chancer, David Gadd, the late John Hood-Williams and Tom Wengraf. Finally, we offer sincere thanks to our interviewees – Ivy, Tommy, Kelly, Ron, Roger, Joyce, Jane, Fran, Linda, Hassan, Phil, Juliet, June, both Anns (pilot and main group) and all the others – for the thoughtful generosity of their participation. We hope we have respected this in the use we have made of their interviewed lives.

CHAPTER I

INTRODUCTION: THE NEED TO DO RESEARCH DIFFERENTLY

What do you, the researcher, assume about a person's capacity to know, remember and tell about themselves? In this book, we argue and illustrate the proposition that social researchers need to revise their assumptions about the nature of that person – the research subject[1] – and that this revision should change their research practices.

Assume that you have to do a piece of research. As an example, let us suppose that you are interested in the fear of crime. Reading the literature, much of which is survey-based, you have learned that women consistently come out as more fearful than men, but there seem to be no satisfactory explanations for this, especially since young men seem more crime-prone. Moreover, you have women friends who claim to be unafraid of crime and you suspect that some of your male friends are more afraid than they are letting on. From this common-sense starting-point you frame your central research questions, namely: (a) what is the meaning of the finding that women are more fearful of crime than men; and (b) (if this finding is valid) why are they?

You then identify a number of female and male acquaintances (of a range of ages because age differences have also been found to be significant) who are willing to be informants to see if you can shed some light on these questions. This poses the problem of how you can find out relevant information from your informants. Do you just ask them directly the question(s) to which you wish to find an answer? If not, why not? How else would you approach them? Would it be feasible to observe them in relevant situations? If you decide on a face-to-face interview is it best to structure it through a series of questions? What should they cover and how many do you need? In other words, just how are you going to produce data which, when analysed, will help answer your starting questions?

Let us assume that you have constructed a series of questions, designed to explore face to face the fearfulness of your male and female respondents. This is the most common qualitative method used in the social sciences. You interview them. What then? Will you believe everything you are told? If not, how will you distinguish between truth and untruth? Even if you believe everything you are told, will you be satisfied that you have been told everything that is relevant? How would you define this, and how would you know? What do you assume about the effect of people's motivations and memory on what they tell you? What will you assume about your effect as interviewer on the answers given? Does your sex, race, age and so on make a difference? Will men talk readily about their fear to a woman or a man, or to neither? How do you know?

Beyond questions of the veracity of the data produced are the questions of their significance. How will you analyse your interviewees' answers to make some overall sense of them, especially when their accounts are littered with contradictions and inconsistencies? If you conclude that Tom is more fearful than he lets on, or that Anna is fearful out of all proportion to the risks she runs, what is informing these judgements? Why might your conclusions be more, or less, reliable than theirs? Can their answers help answer your starting questions, and if so, how? What theories of gender difference and of fear do you apply to your analysis and how?

All these questions faced us when we decided that existing approaches to research into the fear of crime seemed unable to explain satisfactorily the basic finding of women's greater fear of crime. The finding seemed clear enough as it was endlessly reproduced (see below), but its meaning was puzzling given that women apparently are less likely to be victims of crime outside the home. Perhaps the problem lay with the question generally asked ('How safe do you feel walking alone in your neighbourhood after dark?'); perhaps with the truthfulness or otherwise of the answers given; perhaps with the range of unexamined meanings such answers contained; perhaps a mixture of all three. In any event, existing, survey-based research into the fear of crime seemed ill suited to answer the very questions it made visible: 'why' questions and questions about what particular findings mean.

Survey research will do well enough to find out how many locks people have on their doors, or whether they have installed security lights, and other easily measurable factors. But, with something as complex (and hence unquantifiable) as fear, survey research has not been able to answer the 'what', never mind the 'why', of a given person's, or community's, fear of crime. To use another example that interests us, namely, sexuality, survey research might be able to find out how many sexual partners a person has had in a given period (although actually it might signally fail to do so), but it cannot find out what this means, nor why sexual behaviour of whatever kind is engaged in.

If quantitative survey-based research is not up to addressing 'what does this mean' and 'why' questions, it does not follow that the other, qualitative, research tradition has ready answers to such questions. In our experience, it has not. Primarily, this is because of the widespread assumptions in the tradition, by ethnographers, participant observers and interviewers alike, that their participants are 'telling it like it is', that participants know who they are and what makes them tick – what we might call the 'transparent self problem' – and are willing and able to 'tell' this to a stranger interviewer – what we might call the 'transparent account problem'. Neither selves nor accounts are transparent in our view. Treating people's own accounts as unproblematic flies in the face of what is known about people's less clear-cut, more confused and contradictory relationship to knowing and telling about themselves. In everyday informal dealings with each other, we do not take each other's accounts at face value, unless we are totally naïve; we question, disagree, bring in counter-examples, interpret, notice hidden agendas. Research is only a more formalised and systematic way of knowing about people, but in the process it seems to have lost much of the subtlety and complexity that we use, often as a matter of course, in everyday knowing. We need to bring some of this everyday subtlety into the research process.

One of the good reasons for believing what people tell us, as researchers, is a democratic one: who are we to know any better than the participants when it is, after all, their lives? If we are prepared to disagree, modify, select and interpret what they tell us, is this not an example of the kind of power that we, as researchers, have that should be kept in check by being faithful to the voices of those we are researching? Feminists, in their efforts to diminish the power differentials between researcher and researched, have been strong advocates of the principle of giving voice to hitherto voiceless women. But, as Riessman (1993: 8) claims, 'we cannot give voice' since we 'do not have direct access to another's experience. We deal with ambiguous representations of it – talk, text, interaction and interpretation.' If we wish to do justice to the complexity of our subjects an interpretative approach is unavoidable. It can also be fair, democratic and not patronising, as long as this approach to knowing people through their accounts is applied to the researcher as well as the researched; as long as researchers are not seen as neutral vehicles for representing knowledge in an uncontaminated way (sometimes called 'God's eye view' or 'the view from nowhere'). In other words, it is legitimate as long as there is no special objective status that excludes us from being theorised as the same kind of subjects as our informants (albeit in a different position from them).

However, the now widespread recognition of the need to interpret accounts has led to the problem of just how to escape the 'hermeneutical circle' (Denzin, 1989: 141), the idea that there is no end to the interpretative process. If experiences can only ever be ambiguously represented, is interpreting these various representations, rather than the experiences themselves, the only possible activity for researchers? We think not. We think that, though it is far from transparent, there is a relationship between people's ambiguous representations and their experiences. This position is sometimes called 'critical realism'

(Bunge, 1993; Watkins, 1994–5). But, tracking this relationship relies on a particular view of the research subject: one whose inner world is not simply a reflection of the outer world, nor a cognitively driven rational accommodation to it. Rather, we intend to argue for the need to posit research subjects whose inner worlds cannot be understood without knowledge of their experiences in the world, and whose experiences of the world cannot be understood without knowledge of the way in which their inner worlds allow them to experience the outer world. This research subject cannot be known except through another subject; in this case, the researcher. The name we give to such subjects is psychosocial: our justifications for such a starting-point, and the consequent theoretical, methodological and ethical implications for research, constitute the subject matter of our book.

The book's content

In Chapter 2 we continue to work with the example of the fear of crime, showing how the survey research on which this area of enquiry was initially based made a series of unwarranted methodological and theoretical assumptions. However, we argue that qualitative research into the fear of crime has failed, as it has in other areas, to look critically at the assumptions it shares with survey research about the nature of the research subject on whose accounts knowledge about the fear of crime depends. We use the case examples of Roger and Joyce to illustrate how our understanding of psychosocial subjects can explain differences in the fear of crime in two people who share many social characteristics.

Chapter 3 is about producing data through the interview method. It looks closely at our initial failures in a pilot interview and makes the case, as a result, for moving from question- and answer-based interviewing to narrative interviewing. However, the theory of the subject implicit in narrative interviewing leaves no space for what we call the 'defended' subject (understanding the effects of defences against anxiety on people's actions and stories about them). The method that we developed to accommodate the psychoanalytic principles of the defended subject is based on eliciting and paying attention to free association. We illustrate how it works in the case of Jane's opening response in one such interview. In this way we introduce the free-association narrative interview method. Qualitative researchers take seriously the need to understand the role of the interviewer in the production and analysis of data and in this chapter we begin a theme which continues throughout the book, namely, the unconscious intersubjective dynamics in the interview relationship, which we explain and illustrate using concepts such as countertransference, recognition and containment.

Following the focus in Chapter 3 on data production, Chapter 4 is all about data analysis. Here, we take some extended and detailed examples from one family we interviewed (Ivy and two of her adult children, Tommy and Kelly) to demonstrate our approach to analysing unstructured qualitative data. In contrast to the widespread tendency in qualitative research to fragment data by using code and retrieve methods, we illustrate a method based on the principle of working with the whole data and paying attention to links and contradictions within that whole. We demonstrate not only the need for theoretically informed interpretation, but how we do it, based on what principles.

Having given a detailed account of methods of data production and analysis, we turn to the implications that this different approach has for some of the key issues in qualitative research, namely ethics and the generalisability of knowledge derived from case-based analyses. In Chapter 5, we take available ethical guidelines for the conduct of social-science research and assess their appropriateness in three cases chosen from our own research. We demonstrate their inadequacy in this new domain and map out the contours of an alternative approach, based on principles of honesty, sympathy and respect.

In Chapter 6 we examine the tension in our research into the fear of crime between the use of case studies and the need for research to be able to generalise its findings. We show the weaknesses involved in coding and clustering our 37 cases for the purposes of generalisation. We use a series of mini-examples to demonstrate how cases with identical codings were not similar once personal meanings were taken into account and how women's shared risks of sexual assault did not account for their fear of crime. We conclude that generalisations about the fear of crime need to be based on biography as well as demographic factors.

Throughout the book, we conduct our argument using detailed case-study illustrations. In Chapter 7, we demonstrate, through a single, extensive and multifaceted case study of a 24-year-old burglar, Ron, what can be achieved through the free-association narrative interview method, our approach to data analysis and our psychosocial theory of the subject. This is a case study which goes well beyond description and uses and refines theory to provide insights into the importance of Ron's biography and his inner world in understanding his criminal activities. In addition, we address some central issues in qualitative research concerning the role of memory and the possibility of gaining access to truth through interview-based research.

We end with a short Afterword which outlines the difference that adopting our view of the research subject might make to qualitative research.

Note

1   The history of the term 'subject' in this – research methods – context may have come full circle. We use 'subject' not in the tradition of experimental psychology (where the term is criticised, paradoxically, for objectifying the people taking part in research) but in the philosophical sense. Here 'subject' refers to the person and how s/he is theorised.

CHAPTER 2

RESEARCHING THE FEAR OF CRIME

In researching any topic, there are two overarching questions that have to be addressed: *what* is the object of enquiry and *how* can it be enquired into? In respect of the fear of crime, these translate into 'What is the fear of crime?' and 'How can it be measured?' For the sake of simplicity, in what follows we shall refer to 'what'-related questions as *theoretical*, and 'how'-related ones as *methodological*. In research into the fear of crime there have been far more attempts to measure the fear of crime than to ask what it is that is being measured. Although this problem has been recognised by some authors,[1] even these have failed to notice the importance of a further question: namely, *who* is the assumed subject of research? In this respect, research into the fear of crime is typical. As we intend to show during the course of this chapter, the problems this common oversight poses for research are as grave as the failure to define the fear of crime.

'How safe do you feel ...?'

It may seem remarkable now that, without defining what the fear of crime was, early researchers in the field, such as those conducting the first British Crime Survey (Hough and Mayhew, 1983), felt able to measure it. They found that women, especially elderly women, are more fearful of crime than men. Because this finding was 'discovered with monotonous regularity' (Gilchrist et al., 1998), the fearful old lady, afraid to venture out after dark, has become a common stereotype, as the authors of the 1996 British Crime Survey came to bemoan (Mirrlees-Black et al., 1996: 55). Yet, when we remind ourselves of the original source of this knowledge, we find it stems from the answers of large national samples to the following question: 'How safe do you feel walking alone in this area after dark?' Moreover, the answer was required to fit into one of four categories: 'very safe', 'fairly safe', 'a bit unsafe' or 'very unsafe'.

Survey research interviews of this kind, where answers can be quantified on a Likert scale, are so prevalent that their capacity to produce evidence is taken for granted. Mishler's extensive consideration of research interviewing concluded that the 'standard approach to interviewing [the survey interview] is demonstrably inappropriate for and inadequate to the study of the central questions in the social and behavioural sciences' (1986: ix). The main reason for this is because the approach fails to address the way in which respondents' meanings are related to circumstances. Reliance on coding isolated responses strips any remaining context from these responses:

> The problem raised by so radical a decontextualization of the interview at so many different levels ... is that respondents' answers are disconnected from essential socio-cultural grounds of meaning. Each answer is a fragment removed from both its setting in the organized discourse of the interview and from the life setting of the respondent. (Mishler, 1986: 23)

Of course, these responses, duly coded, have to be reassembled so as to make sense of them. However, 'when these [fragmented] responses are assembled into different subgroups by age, gender and the like, the results are artificial aggregates that have no direct representation in the real world' (Mishler, 1986: 26). These are the processes which have generated the findings about gender and age differences in the fear of crime. As Josselson (1995: 32) puts it: 'when we aggregate people, treating diversity as error variable, in search of what is common to all, we often learn about what is true of no one in particular.'

Another way of examining the problems with survey research questions is to look at the methodological and theoretical assumptions underlying them. Let us look at the assumptions about the fear of crime that underpinned the framing of the fear of crime question in the British Crime Survey (BCS).

Methodological assumptions

- It is a basic assumption in much social-science research that if the words used are the same, and if they are communicated in the same manner, they will mean the same thing to numerous people in a sample. On this principle a great deal hangs: the possibility of reliability, and the validity of quantification, comparison and generalisation.
- If the same words do not guarantee the same meanings, the 'alone in the dark in a public space' scenario of the BCS raises some interesting questions about what the scenario conjures up differently for different groups. For young men, it might suggest fighting; for older people, mugging; for women, sexual assault.
- Abstract and closed questions of this sort delimit a horizon of thought. If you do not frame a respondent's agenda in these formless terms (Ferraro and LaGrange, 1987), they will talk about specific crimes which they fear: burglary or mugging or car theft. Women often talk about their fear of rape, for example (Pain, 1993).

Theoretical assumptions

- By asking about safety, but making claims about fear, the research is assuming a relationship between these two which is not spelled out; that is, a relationship which is taken for granted. It looks as if safety and fear are assumed to be opposite ends of a continuum, where feeling safe is equivalent to not feeling fearful and vice versa.
- The scenario presented is not one depicting crime but one in which some potential threat to safety must be imagined. Fear of some imagined threat is thus assumed to correspond to fear of crime. But 'threat' can correspond to a whole range of fears and anxieties. For example, Freud suggested that three images define human anxiety: being alone, in the dark, and in the presence of a stranger.[2] The BCS's question on the fear of crime reproduces the first two of these and the third would be represented by the imagined criminal. In conjuring up these images, then, the question may be eliciting more about general anxiety than the fear of crime.
- By asking people to imagine themselves 'walking alone','after dark', a frightening scenario is depicted. Does this scenario derive from commonplace situations that people routinely find themselves in? Not really, when people are more commonly in groups and under street lighting. It is the stuff of horror fiction, though, and nightmares.
- The generalised framing of the question assumes that a person's feeling of fear is consistent over time. That is to say, it forces someone to claim, in effect, that every time, or never, they feel safe or unsafe, irrespective of contingent events or mood.

As we suggested earlier, these sorts of methodological and theoretical criticisms of existing survey-based work in this area are now more common (for example, Farrall et al., 1997: 662):

> Taken together, these criticisms suggest that crime surveys ignore the meaning of events for respondents; turn 'processes' into 'events'; neglect that the fear of crime can be a multi-faceted phenomenon; poorly conceptualise the fear of crime; ignore important contextual variables (such as time and space); greatly influence the reported incidence of the fear of crime and rely too heavily on respondents' recall.

While we agree with this conclusion, these criticisms of the 'what' and the 'how' of survey-based research are not accompanied by an equally critical look at the 'who' of such research. It is this blindness to the issue of what research subject is being assumed which compromises not only efforts to develop a 'more sensitive qualitative understanding' of the fear of crime (Gilchrist et al., 1998: 296), but all the other attempts by qualitative researchers to rectify the problems of quantitative, survey-based approaches in this field.

'Telling it like it is'

In response to these limitations of survey and other questionnaire research in addressing questions of meaning and causality, many researchers have looked to qualitative research. For example, researchers influenced by feminism, who criticised early work on the fear of crime for not taking into account the routine sexual harassment of women or the particular vulnerability of women to rape, often used in-depth or semi-structured face-to-face interviews to ask women (and men in some cases) about their fears.[3] One result of such feminist critiques of traditional 'scientific' methods was a situation in which 'it began to be assumed that only qualitative methods, especially the in-depth, face-to face interview, could really count in feminist terms and generate useful knowledge' (Maynard, 1994: 12). More generally, face-to-face interviewing has become the most common type of qualitative research method used in order to find out about people's experiences in context, and the meanings these hold. Considerable effort has been directed to adapting the traditional interview format so that it is adequate to these purposes (see Mishler, 1986; Berg and Smith, 1988; Maynard and Purvis, 1994). But, despite the energy expended, the idea that an interviewee can 'tell it like it is' still remains the unchallenged starting-point for most of this qualitative, interview-based research. One revealing effect of this is that the questions the interviewer asks in order to get respondents to 'tell it like it is' are often not considered worthy of mention.

For example, Gilchrist and colleagues' (1998) own qualitative follow-up to their critique of the survey-based literature on the fear of crime (Farrall et al., 1997) has several pages of men and women, the fearful and the fearless, talking about their fear of crime. We learn that these extracts have been taken 'from 64 qualitative interviews with (equal numbers of) men and women in Glasgow' (Gilchrist et al., 1998: 286). We learn also that, allowed to speak for themselves, the importance of the gender divide diminishes since 'there are striking similarities between men's and women's fears about crime' (1998: 296). But what we never learn is what it is that respondents are responding to: how they were invited to tell about their fear of crime.

This failure to examine the role of the interviewer's questions in the process suggests that they believed that the problematic assumptions that they identified in relation to survey-based research disappear when the 'meaning of events for respondents' is taken into account. We cannot agree. Even if no theoretical assumptions are being made about the fear of crime since this is left for respondents to define, and even if the question asked is no longer a closed one, at least one problematic methodological assumption of survey research still applies. This is that words mean the same thing to the interviewer and the interviewees. In other words, the researchers, in taking this for granted, are still assuming that a shared meaning attaches to words: that the question asked will be the one that is understood.

This assumption relies on a discredited theory of the transparency of language. Current theories of language and communication stress that any kind of account can only be a mediation of reality. Hence there can be no guarantees that different people will share the same meanings when it comes to making sense of an interviewee's account. In taking into account the context of the interview, clearly the role of the interviewer is a central mediation in the making of meaning. A further reason for assuming shared meanings between interviewer and interviewee is connected with the taken-for-granted notion of the subject of research in qualitative research. In essence, this is the same subject as that assumed by survey researchers.

A shared subject

So far, we have pointed out some of the theoretical and methodological assumptions built into the wording of the original fear of crime question in the BCS, and shown how the shift to qualitative research surmounts some, but not all, of these problems. The similarity between qualitative and quantitative approaches becomes evident when we focus specifically on the presumed subject in each research tradition. The subject assumed by the BCS question and by all survey-type research assumes that the respondent is one who:

- shares meanings with the researcher;
- is knowledgeable about his/her experience (in this case an emotional experience of feeling safe);
- can access this through an imaginary scenario (which he or she may or may not have experienced);
- can capture it satisfactorily in a single concept;
- can make distinctions in amount, such as the difference between 'fairly safe' and 'a bit unsafe'.

The fact that respondents routinely do provide answers as part of their cooperation in the research does not validate these assumptions.

Taking a research subject's account as a faithful reflection of 'reality' similarly assumes that a person is one who:

- shares meanings with the researcher;
- is knowledgeable about him or herself (his or her actions, feelings and relations);

- can access the relevant knowledge accurately and comprehensively (that is, has accurate memory);
- can convey that knowledge to a stranger listener;
- is motivated to tell the truth.

In short, whatever their other differences on the 'what' and 'how' of research, on the matter of the 'who' of research, quantitative and qualitative research traditions converge. This is one central reason why research into the fear of crime cannot resolve the two issues it persistently raises, namely:

- Is the fear of crime realistic or irrational?
- Are differences in the fear of crime explained by social factors?

Is the fear of crime realistic or irrational?

The finding that women's and older people's fear of crime was greater than that of men and younger people, even though their risks were less (the fear–risk paradox), was generally greeted with the response that women's and older people's fear of crime was therefore irrational (Hough and Mayhew, 1983). This interpretation took the relative fearlessness of men and younger people as normative and rational. The rational–irrational dichotomy is pervasive well beyond social science and is indicative of the widespread assumption of a 'rational' subject, where deviations are then regarded as irrational. The policy response was to try to encourage people to become more rational by giving them information about 'real' risks which would help them to become less fearful (Home Office Standing Conference on Crime Prevention, 1989). This response reveals another assumption about the human subject: that rationality includes the ability to calculate the probability of risks and make decisions on this basis (about safe times to go out or when to catch a taxi home rather than walk). These kinds of capacities are central to the idea of the information-processing individual which is at the heart of cognitive psychology's and social science's assumptions about the human subject.[4]

When this interpretation of irrationality was challenged it was to advance a realist model of the fear of crime; that is, it defended the rationality of various groups' higher fear. Jones et al. (1986) argued that people living in certain kinds of neighbourhoods based their fear on real risks, a fact that was obscured in the averaging of experiences in large national samples like those of the BCS. Stanko (1990) has pointed out the real risks for women of harassment, assault and rape by men in public and domestic spaces. She argues that risk calculation is sensibly about the seriousness of the potential threat (notably rape) as well as its probability. Later, realist explanations have explored a new paradox, namely, that women are at much greater risk of physical and sexual assault in their own homes than in public spaces, but that their fear does not reflect this (Pain, 1995: 590). In this debate, the rational, information-processing subject (whose 'other' is irrational) has prevailed to the extent that none of these authors has tried to theorise what might lie behind the so-called irrationality of people's fear – the 'method in their madness'.

Are differences in the fear of crime explained by social factors?

While sociologists and criminologists assume a rational, information-processing, psychological subject when trying to explain the fear–risk paradox, they are happiest assuming a socially constructed subject; that is, a subject who is largely determined by demographic factors. This dovetails with their reliance on statistical analyses which divide respondents into demographically based groups: class, sex, race, age and neighbourhood type being the most commonly used.[5] When differences are found, for example, between men and women, old and young, or different ethnic groups, these dominate the interpretation. Not surprisingly, then, the fear of crime debate has been fixated on these differences.

More recently, it has been acknowledged that, whatever it is that social factors explain, it falls far short of a complete explanation. This is because, for example, the differences in fear levels between the sexes 'is not that startling' (Gilchrist et al., 1998: 283) and, as we saw earlier, 'there are as many similarities across gender groups as differences between them' (1998: 296). This 'individual–social paradox' (how individuals come to have experiences supposedly at odds with the norm for their social position, the fearless woman, the fearful man etc.), begs the question of how social differences are reflected in an individual's fear of crime.[6]

The premise of a socially constructed subject, albeit one capable of rationally or irrationally judging risks, makes it impossible to encapsulate fully the diversity of individuals' lived experience. This becomes increasingly apparent when methods other than survey methods are used, as Gilchrist and colleagues (1998: 296) found: 'We now know *that* some women are not fearful, and *that* some men are fearful: yet we are some way from knowing *why* this should be, and we are a long way from knowing whether or not fear (or fearlessness) encompasses shared meanings.' Despite their insightful criticisms of survey-based work, and despite their efforts to supplement these shortcomings with qualitative research, this rather forlorn conclusion is, we suggest, the inevitable result of the failure to problematise the subjects of research (researchers as well as researched). Once methods allow for individuals to express what they mean, theories not only have to address the status of these meanings for that person and their understanding by the researcher, but they must also take into account the uniqueness of individuals. What such a theory of the subject entails is addressed in the next section.

Understanding subjects as psychosocial

We have identified two persistent issues in the sets of assumptions that are made about people who are fearful of crime: how realistic or irrational are these subjects; and to what extent are they explained by their shared social circumstances, as opposed to something irreducibly unique to them as individuals? Both of these questions are central to how we are trying to understand the subject as 'psychosocial' (that is, simultaneously psychic and social). In what follows we will be more specific about what we mean by these terms and their interrelation, using two case examples, Roger and Joyce, from our research into the fear of crime, to illustrate our approach.

The turn to language and the discursive subject

If people's fear of crime has really grown disproportionately to their risk of crime, what intervenes between people's risks of criminal victimisation and how these are experienced? In the past few decades there has been a massive shift of emphasis in social theory away from assumptions that the external world can be apprehended accurately through the senses and via information-processing mechanisms to one which claims that it is impossible to know that world directly. This is because everything we know about it is mediated by language, and the meanings which are available through language never represent the world neutrally. This shift is variously referred to as the shift from 'world' to 'word', the 'turn to language' or the 'hermeneutic turn' (that is, a move to emphasise meanings and their interpretation).

How then do meanings affect people's fear of crime? We use the term 'discourse' in preference to 'language' because it refers beyond language to sets of organised meanings (which can include images as well as words) on a given theme. The term 'discourse' has been used to emphasise the organised way in which meanings cohere around an assumed central proposition, which gives them their value and significance. For example, the 'permissive discourse' (Hollway, 1989) refers to a central proposition about sex based on the belief that sex with many partners can be both pleasurable and harmless. People's claims and practices refer to this, whether in agreement or not, as one of the dominant contemporary Western sets of meanings about sex.

Discourses of crime are widespread. They may be met with in the form of media news, media fiction or local talk of crime. Commonly, victims are represented as defenceless and hapless and, since these discourses are everywhere, people become fearful, it is argued, as a result of imagining themselves in these positions. This is one explanation of the finding that people's fear of crime has grown disproportionately to their real risks of victimisation. It is easy to extend this argument to account for women's and older people's greater fear of crime since these crime discourses typically position women and older people as the vulnerable ones, whereas the criminal is usually depicted as a young man. A label for this idea – of how people are formed by discursive representations – is 'the discursive subject'. It is one version of a socially constructed subject.

Roger, fear and crime discourses

It follows from this line of argument that being fearful of crime could be explained by being positioned in a fear of crime discourse.[7] If this were the case, however, there would be no variation within a group, say, of old women, yet not all the old women we interviewed were fearful, nor all the young men fearless (see Gilchrist et al., 1998).[8] We need to account for individual differences in the way in which people make sense of the available information; that is, the discourses or systems of meaning within which they may be positioned. We will first use the example of Roger, a 58-year-old unemployed man living on a high-crime council estate, and look at his fear in relation to crime discourses and then try to make sense of why he, in particular, comes to fear crime, unlike some other men of his age on the same estate. To understand his fearfulness, we shall argue that we need to attend to his particular biography and how this relates to the question of his investments in crime discourses. By investments, we mean someone's desires and anxieties, probably not conscious or intentional, which motivate the specific positions they take up and the selection of accounts through which they portray themselves.

Roger spends much of his time hanging over his gate, watching local comings and goings. He sees the local kids joy-riding or transporting stolen parts in carrier bags, and hears stories of local burglaries and police impotence, but he has not personally been a victim of crime.[9] He puts this down to knowing the local kids, and they him. He also mentions his good house-dog, and we could add that he has never owned a car. He is, none the less, quite fearful. When on his own at home he is easily startled ('least little noise, I'd jump, me') and doesn't sleep well. When opening the door late at night he would always 'put catch on and open it just to 'ave a look to make sure who it were'. Before going on holiday, he leaves the TV, video and his wife's jewellery with his daughter, despite the dog remaining in the house ('you 'ear 'em doing things to dogs ... best to be safe than sorry').

Though he is not frightened of walking round the estate after dark, ''cos I've been brought up round 'ere', he wouldn't now cut through local woods or parks after dark, since he heard of a man being mugged by three Jamaicans 'about eight year ago' while doing so. Nor would he walk around certain areas, though he would have done so when young, ''cos there were no – I know it's 'orrible to keep saying it – but there were no coloureds hardly down there then.' 'Coloureds' are not the only group to which he links the decline of the estate: there's 'some right riff-raff up 'ere na ... you've got Scots ... and all sorts living ... up on [the rough end] ... there's ... gypsies on. Mind you, like I say, they 'aven't done owt to me, but I don't know I care for 'em much.'

He regards the pub as unsafe, though it used to be 'great' when he first moved on to the estate, full of 'rough and ready' lads.[10] This 'then' and 'now' contrast recurred throughout the transcript: when they first moved on to the estate it was 'smashing': 'tha could 'ave left thee doors open or owt ... you never got no trouble then.'

There is in all this a disjunction between Roger's knowledge of the mundane reality of local crime (joy-riding, fencing stolen goods, burglaries) and the lurid tales of vicious violence that he avidly recounts: 'you read in paper na, they'd kick you in for five quid or less, won't they' (a reference to an 80-year-old man murdered by two teenagers in the city centre). Why do such media-based stories resonate with him? Why does his local knowledge not serve to put these violent events in proportion, as it did with others, to recognise them as the rare events they are, especially on the estate where he lives?

Roger's investments in the past and patriarchal authority

To make full sense of Roger's fear of crime, then, we need to explore why contemporary tales of murder and mayhem animate him despite the contrary evidence of his own experience, and how these are connected to his perception of the decline of the estate. The past he harks back to was certainly not free from crime, nor violence, but it was, he insists, controlled. When he talks of fights, he remembers that, unlike today, they were never allowed to get out of hand: 'nobody would join in and kick everybody in. Two lads who were gonna fight, they'd fight', but would be stopped if one were getting 'a good 'iding'. Today 'they don't, they use glasses, knives and everything, don't they ... Now when you pick up paper or read news or owt – every time there's a fight, somebody's been knifed or summat ... Same wi' – wi' guns in' it?'

What kept violence and misbehaviour in check then was patriarchal authority: 'when I were a kid – only brought up rough and ready, but daren't do owt wrong ... tha'd 'ave got – well tha'd 'ave got pasted – got a right 'ammering'; a philosophy that extended from beltings at home and canings at school to 'glove across ear'ole' from the local policeman if caught playing football in the street. Such harshness allegedly produced respect: 'though you were only rough and ready, you respected 'em' (your parents). This was despite hating his dad (''e were cruel old sod'), especially for his treatment of Roger's mother (' 'e were 'orrible wi' 'er'). Now patriarchal authority and respect have disappeared: you see 'bits of kids at 13, 14 or 15 walking around estate at 12 o'clock at night and that ... In my days I wouldn't 'ave been allowed.' Roger can only watch helplessly when local joy-riders 'go past and do two fingers to ya' because his wife won't let him report them for fear 'they'll come and put all your windows through.'

How is Roger making sense of his fears about crime? The main discourse appears quite familiar: its themes are the failure of law and order, a decline of respect for authority in young people, and the consequent rise in criminality around him. These claims rely on comparisons with a better time, and Roger, like many older people, constructs his past, as well as his current life, within this discourse.

On the face of it, it is surprising that Roger frightens himself by imagining the worst. It may well be true that certain things are worse than they were; that certain kinds of violence are more gratuitous or less controlled. But we still need to explain why Roger (unlike Joyce, as we show below) is drawn to this reading of the present and not a more nuanced account. We believe that it is only possible to understand people's use of particular crime discourses by attending to their personal investment in them. What is it about a given discourse, like that in which the past constitutes a 'golden age', that attracts some, but not all, of us? In Roger's case, we will show how this investment is connected to his identity, and how this can be enhanced or made more secure, rather than undermined or threatened, by the self that it is possible to produce in the accounts that one gives of oneself and one's life. To do this we need first to know a little more about Roger's life.

At 58, Roger is a prematurely aged man in poor health. Married, with four married children and 11 grandchildren, he and his wife have lived on the respectable side of the estate for 26 years, moving twice in that time. The first-born of five, he was brought up on a 'rough and ready' nearby local estate by a strict, wife-beating father who he ' 'ated', and a mother who he 'thought the world of'. At 19, he got 'right satisfaction' out of giving his dad 'a good 'iding' for all his years of wife-battering and other cruelties. He got employment as a miner.

At 21, a pit-shaft accident kept him off work for two years, leaving him temporarily depressed (although electric shock treatment left him 'as right as rain after') and permanently disabled. Though he did do labouring jobs subsequently, since 'light work' never paid enough, he was laid off in his late thirties and has never worked since.

A conflict in his account suggests why he is invested in an idealised version of parts of his past. On the one hand, he hated his father for his cruel exercise of power over the family. On the other, he 'respected' him for the exercise of authority (also through brutal means). A discourse of a 'golden age' when patriarchal authority still worked legitimates, and thereby mitigates, an aspect of his past which caused him suffering. It also allows him to secure a moment when patriarchal authority counted for something. This is in contrast to its loss in the present, especially in his own life, where his ability to exercise patriarchal control has been brief and limited. Whatever control he might have exercised as an adult man was quickly undermined by the disabling accident, depression, an upsetting failure to make National Service and a subsequent work life dictated by the Labour Exchange ('them days, they said "go for a job" and you went'). This was cut short by the onset of recession in the 1970s, and then by serious health problems.

Despite the decline of patriarchal authority signalled by these social changes, he – like other men – still expected to exercise that same authority in his own home as his father had. As a family man he was strict, but times had changed. Once he hit his daughter (the one time she was late home): 'I grabbed 'er and knocked 'er through 'edge, didn't I.' The result was that he felt ' 'orrible' and his wife 'went mad'. As a grandad, he is reduced to saying what he'd have done to his 16-year-old granddaughter who stopped overnight somewhere other than where she'd said she would: 'if that 'ad been my … know it's only my granddaughter … I'd 'ave got 'old of 'er an' pasted 'er.' Even his imaginings of exercising such power are faced with a changed reality when his wife reminds him: 'you don't do them things today, you've got to give and take.' Even as an old-established resident of the estate, his age-based authority counts for nothing. He feels he can only endure impotently the cheeky disrespect of joy-riders. Given this lack of control, it is small wonder that Roger's identity is so invested in a nostalgia for a 'golden age' of traditional, patriarchal authority.

We are trying to demonstrate through this example that it is because of his investments that Roger takes up the particular theme about crime that he does, that of a lost 'golden age' of law and order based on respect for patriarchal authority. This use of a common discourse is rendered unique by being inflected with meanings in which he is invested because of the tensions and conflicts in his own biography. Paradoxically (given that the effect is to amplify his fear), the pain of his experiences can be rendered more benign by adopting this discourse. The meanings are both common and unique, social and biographical, discursive and defended. In what follows, we will explore further the nature of these investments, theorising them as unconscious, defensive and intersubjective.

Klein, anxiety and the defended subject

We have argued that Roger had an identity investment in his positioning in this particular crime discourse. We now need to explore how to theorise such an identity or 'self'. In particular, we need to show how conflict, suffering and threats to self operate on the psyche in ways that affect people's positioning and investment in certain discourses rather than others. This will help us to understand the workings of the psyche and the social simultaneously. For this purpose we must explain our theory of the 'defended' subject.

We have suggested that Roger's investment in a discourse of an idealised past serves a defensive function: it legitimates and therefore mitigates his experiences of his father's brutality, and more generally of the harshness of his earlier life. In so doing it serves to defend his self. This argument assumes that threats to the self create anxiety, and indeed this is a fundamental proposition in psychoanalytic theory, where anxiety is viewed as being inherent in the human condition. For psychoanalysis, anxiety precipitates defences against the threats it poses to the self and these operate at a largely unconscious level. The shared starting-point of all the different schools of psychoanalytic thought is this idea of a dynamic unconscious which defends against anxiety and significantly influences people's actions, lives and relations.

We use the theories of psychoanalyst Melanie Klein (1988a, b) about how the self is forged out of unconscious defences against anxiety. Her account starts at the very beginning of life. According to Klein, early experience is dominated by anxiety in the face of the infant's state of complete dependency. Because the infant has no conception of time, it is incapable of anticipating the satisfaction of a feed when it is feeling the frustration of hunger. Thus it experiences polarised emotions of 'bad' (when hungry) and 'good' (when fed). Gradually, the infant becomes capable of recognising the breast, and later the mother, as a whole object containing both the capacity to fulfil and frustrate. However, the bad and good will, when necessary, be kept mentally separate for defensive purposes in order to protect the good from the bad.

The concept of splitting originated in Freud's view of the mind as conflicted and capable of producing inconsistent thoughts and beliefs. In a late paper (Freud, 1938), he described the way in which the mind could adopt two separate points of view. Klein's work on splitting of the object developed this, emphasising how objects are often given unrealistically good and bad characteristics. Later Klein emphasised the splitting of the ego, where parts of the self that are feared as bad are split off through projection and usually identified as belonging to an outside object (or person) (Hinshelwood, 1991: 433–4). This splitting of objects into good and bad is the basis for what Klein terms the 'paranoid-schizoid' position; a position to which we may all resort in the face of self-threatening occurrences because it permits us to believe in a good object, on which we can rely, uncontaminated by 'bad' threats which have been split off and located elsewhere.

The discourse through which Roger expresses his fear of crime is consistent with a paranoid-schizoid splitting of good and bad in two striking ways. The first is the historical splitting between then and now by which an idealised estate is split off into the past, leaving a denigrated estate in the present characterised by the breakdown of traditional authority. The second is the splitting of people into groups of 'us' and 'them': splitting between people like Roger and 'others' ('coloureds', Scots, gypsies). This locates the bad (danger, threat and criminality) in people who are not his kind. His kind (and himself) can thereby be experienced as good. Following this logic, these splittings would unconsciously serve to protect Roger's self in his current circumstances, the responsibility for which he can locate elsewhere.

In this notion of unconscious defences against anxiety, Klein departs radically from the assumption that the self[11] is a single unit, with unproblematic boundaries separating it from the external world of objects (both people and things). Her proposition (based on clinical work) is that these defences against anxiety are intersubjective, that is, they come into play in relations between people. The separation of good and bad (splitting) is achieved through the unconscious projection (putting out) and introjection (taking in) of mental objects. We have illustrated this idea of unconscious intersubjectivity in Roger's account.

However, according to Klein, the paranoid-schizoid position is not the only way in which people face a threatening world. In contrast, the depressive position involves the acknowledgement that good and bad can be contained in the same object. Being able to recognise the mother who both fulfils and frustrates is the earliest example. This can be a hard position to sustain when faced with external or internal threats to the self. Then the good needs to be preserved, at the cost of reality if necessary. We all move between these positions. We sometimes react in a paranoid-schizoid fashion and split off the bad. At other times, or in a different area of our life, we are able to respond from the depressive position and acknowledge the mixture of good and bad in the same object, person or group.

For example, the fact that Roger felt ''orrible' and his wife 'went mad' on the only occasion he hit his daughter suggests a capacity for empathy more compatible with an ambivalent than a split relationship to his father's early cruelty; that is, an ability to keep simultaneously in mind both the (respected) authority and the (hated) cruelty, and not simply idealise the former split off from the latter. This reading is reinforced by his willingness to respond to the new, non-patriarchal discourse articulated by his wife: 'you don't do them things today.' This evidence of Roger's ambivalent, more depressive, relationship to his past means that our argument about Roger's defensive splitting should be understood as something both context and content specific; that is, produced in the interview context in relation to the fear of crime, not as a general characteristic of Roger's defensive organisation; and as tendential rather than absolute. None the less, different people will be characterised by a predominance of one or the other defensive organisation – the paranoid-schizoid and depressive – as their typical response.

Joyce, crime and the depressive position

Among our 37 interviewees, Joyce (who you will meet again in Chapter 6) was an example of someone who, in the area of fear of crime, seemed to be responding from the depressive position; that is, she was mostly able to acknowledge good and bad in the same object. Here we illustrate briefly her ability to acknowledge a fairly threatening reality without splitting.

Joyce, aged 36, was born in the same house in which she now lives with her four children, on the rough end of the same high-crime estate as Roger. Her husband left three years ago. Although her brother is living with her temporarily and she has a man 'friend' who sometimes stays, she has become accustomed to being on her own in the house, all the more so since the children spend a proportion of their time with their father. Her history of criminal victimisation, like Roger's, is low: the lawn mower and two children's bikes were taken from her garden shed (which she had forgotten to lock up). Unlike Roger, she is not fearful: 'I don't think I've been unsafe ... [or] felt unsafe.' Despite her worries about crime, drugs and her children getting in with 'riff-raff', her own identity and that of her children does not depend, as does Roger's, on splitting the estate of her childhood and the current situation. In the middle of boarded-up windows and stolen scrap metal in front gardens, her house and garden are immaculate, her children well behaved. Her response to the estate's problems is: 'I'm gonna show everybody that good does come off this estate.'

Joyce believed that her safety from crime depended on the fact that she and her large family were local and known and the local criminal ethic was that you don't steal from those like yourself. This principle, however, appeared to be under threat from local drug addicts. She knows this because drugs are the reason for her nephew, who lives locally, having 'gone off the rails'. Her feelings of safety, depending as they did on the belief in the local criminal ethic, were threatened by the theft from her garden shed. In what follows, we can see the defensive struggle between her wish to split off bad criminals as outsiders and her acknowledgement of a more ambivalent reality. She wished that the thief had been a non-local because she was disturbed by the threat a local posed to her local identity: 'When I were robbed, I was 'urt ... I just thought, right the rotten bastards ... I knew that me shed were robbed by someone round 'ere';[12] 'it'd 'ave been better for me if the person that robbed me would 'ave been one of the newcomers.' However, she manages to minimise the threat to her identity of criminals being local by emphasising their good side: 'Even your ... burglars what we 'ave round 'ere ... they're big softies, honestly ... Two of biggest thieves round 'ere ... they used to be in my year at school ... When me 'usband left ... they were smashing.' In her case, her investment in these local connections protect Joyce from constructing a dangerous 'criminal other', which could provide a receptacle for her fears. However, she does not identify with the criminals since she has worked hard for what she has got: 'to know that the person that robbed me ... knew that to pay for them two bikes ... besides my job, I worked at a ... factory for three months.'

There is, then, a fair bit of evidence that Joyce's estimation of risk is quite realistic. She does not deny the problem, and even recognised, like Roger, that things have got worse.[13] But she is able to make certain distinctions and thereby avoids amplifying the problem: 'There's always been crime, but it's never been as bad as what it is now ... I've never honestly 'eard of anybody round 'ere being mugged ... I don't think it's as bad as what people make it out to be.' We believed this to be a fairly balanced and realistic view of local crime, and thus indicative of the depressive position being accessible to Joyce in this arena. There are threats to her identity involved in facing this reality, however, as Kleinian theory would predict: 'I don't want to ... know about [drugs] ... I just don't like to think of it in area.' Since this is her greatest fear for her own children (it has happened to her sister's son), it is threatening to contemplate.

Further evidence of Joyce's moves between a depressive and a paranoid-schizoid position came in response to the question 'Is there anything you're frightened of?' She replied 'I know this is awful to say it, but blacks in area frighten me. Not that I'm frightened of 'em as such, 'cos when I went to school we'd got lots of coloureds in our class. But they do frighten me ... I don't know why they frighten me because probably they're … nice people', and she went on to give an example of a 'smashing' neighbour of hers who is black. In this sequence, she started by splitting off characteristics to be feared in generalised black others and then engaged with the reality of the familiar and safe black neighbour. In a similar move, Joyce identified 'lone parent families' as spoiling the estate and then qualified this by pointing out her own status and asserting that it's not about being a single mother, but about how you bring up your children. In both cases she was momentarily taking up a position in a common discourse which would afford her a ready-made, but unrealistic (because split) set of meanings about crime. In both cases, she modified this discourse from her own experience of local reality.

Overview of Roger and Joyce as psychosocial subjects

To illustrate our ideas about psychosocial subjects, we chose two people, Roger and Joyce, who share many social characteristics. Although dissimilar in age, they both come from big, local families and have both spent most of their lives on the same high-crime estate. Yet their fear of crime is very different and, to some extent, counter-intuitive: Joyce, living alone on the rougher (and arguably riskier) end of the estate, is less fearful than Roger, who lives with his wife on the more respectable end. However, by positing them as biographically unique 'defended subjects', we have produced an understanding of differences between people that are not explicable by a theory of a discursive subject. The idea of a defended subject shows how subjects invest in discourses when these offer positions which provide protections against anxiety and therefore supports to identity. When ambivalent feelings about the same mental object can be acknowledged (like Joyce's way of regarding 'blacks'), investment in a discourse – here a racist discourse – is moderated (unlike in Roger's case).

We have chosen the cases of Roger and Joyce partly in order to unsettle gender stereotypes about fearful women and fearless men. The differences between them can also be used to reflect back on the distinction made in the literature on the fear of crime between individuals' fears being 'rational' or 'irrational', which we discussed above. Our approach transcends this distinction because it can offer a sustained theoretical account of defences against anxiety by which both rationality and irrationality can be explained. Within this approach, rationality depends on a capacity to acknowledge the mixed good and bad characteristics of the external world without compromising reality by internal defensive needs which distort it through splitting.

In our cases, Roger's fear of crime appeared to be more irrational, where Joyce's could be regarded as largely (with oscillations) rational. However, Roger's so-called irrationality is rational to the extent that it serves more pressing unconscious self-protective needs than the need not to frighten himself with images of murder and mayhem. This is the 'method in his madness'.[14]

In this account, unlike some psychoanalytic usages, anxiety is not treated simply as a psychological characteristic. Though it is a feature of individuals, it is not reducible to psychology: anxiety and the defences which it precipitates are complex responses to events and people in the social world, both present and past. Defences against anxiety affect the discourses through which people perceive crime and this affects people's actions. The concept of an anxious, defended subject is simultaneously psychic and social. It is psychic because it is a product of a unique biography of anxiety-provoking life-events and the manner in which they have been unconsciously defended against. It is social in three ways: first, because such defensive activities affect and are affected by discourses (systems of meaning which are a product of the social world); secondly, because the unconscious defences that we describe are intersubjective processes (that is, they affect and are affected by others); and, thirdly, because of the real events in the external, social world which are discursively and defensively appropriated. It is this psychosocial conception of the subject which we believe is most compatible with a serious engagement in researching the 'what', 'how' and 'who' of issues such as the fear of crime and sexuality.

Summary

- We argued that traditional survey research into the fear of crime is based on a series of unwarranted methodological and theoretical assumptions; namely, that the fear of crime is a single entity that can be accessed through one, hypothetical, closed question. However, although qualitative research into the fear of crime aims to give voice to respondents, it continues to assume shared meanings.

- It was concluded that both research traditions fail to problematise the research subject who is seen, in consequence, as either socially constructed and/or rationally driven.

- The idea of the psychosocial subject (combining the ideas of the discursive subject and the defended subject) explained why some, but not all, from particular social categories might be fearful of crime.

- Applying the idea of psychosocial subjects, we explained why the less-at-risk Roger was more fearful of crime than Joyce.

Notes

1   Notably Ferraro and LaGrange (1987), Sparks (1992), Ferraro (1995) and, most recently, Farrall et al. (1997).

2   Bowlby cites Freud, who classified as basic phobias (i.e. irrational fears) the three elements: 'alone', 'in the dark', 'without a familiar person, or rather with an unknown one' (1970/1: 83).

3   See Junger (1987) and Stanko (1990) for critiques of the early research into the fear of crime for not taking into account the routine sexual harassment of women, and Riger et al. (1978: 278) on the particular vulnerability of women to rape. Stanko (1990), Stanko and Hobdell (1993) and Gilchrist et al. (1998) used in-depth or semi-structured face-to-face interviews to ask either men, or women and men, about their fears.

4   See Mary Douglas (1986) for a thorough critique of these assumptions.

5   Nowadays, the number of social categories into which respondents could be grouped – sexual orientation (at least three), particular disabilities, specific ethnicities, etc. – has grown so large that sociology is faced with the problem of the et cetera clause. Moreover, since each of these groups can cross-cut or intersect with each other, there is no mathematical limit to the number of groups imaginable (Hood-Williams, personal communication).

6   Addressing a different problem, but recognising the same paradox, Kroger concludes that 'the mechanisms by which individuals in their different identity statuses create their own life contexts within the broader socio-historical milieu await further description' (1993: 160).

7   Are people 'positioned by' available discourses or do they 'take up positions' in them? A fundamental philosophical disagreement about the nature and extent of people's agency is contained in this question. It is often referred to as 'structure–agency' dualism. The subject we referred to earlier as 'socially constructed' is either seen as one whose identity is more or less determined by external structures or one whose meanings are more or less determined by external discourses.

8   These within-group variations only appear in statistical analyses of survey data in the size of statistically significant differences. Thus we depend on other methods to give meaningful access to them.

9   However, his daughter, who lives on the estate, has had golf clubs and a lawn mower stolen from a garden shed, and his wife was mugged, off the estate, some eight years ago by 'coloured 'uns'.

10   Roger's constant, almost mantra-like, use of the term 'rough and ready' to describe aspects of his past appears to hint at a more contradictory reality: 'rough' seems to be an acknowledgement of something less than ideal, even as the term 'ready' (willing) seems to cast such aspects, overall, in a positive light.

11   Klein consistently used the term 'ego' and never the self. In this book, we have tried to use the term 'self' consistently to overcome problems with overlapping and rather generalised usages of such terms as self, subjectivity, individual and ego. This does mean leaving aside certain theoretical niceties, for example in Klein's use of the term 'ego'.

12   She was right: in three days she was told who it was, along with an offer of the goods back.

13   Her non-use of a 'golden age' discourse can partly be accounted for by age: Roger has an extra 22 years to look back on. However, this does not obviate the need for a psychological account in addition to this social one.

14   Although we interviewed both Roger and Joyce (and our other interviewees) twice, our knowledge of their lives is too limited to answer fully the question as to the origins of their particular defensive organisations (in relation to the fear of crime). However, since people split that which is too painful to acknowledge or too difficult to assimilate, taking up paranoid-schizoid rather than depressive positions will tend to be associated with trauma. Since Roger's early life, as recounted, seems to have been more traumatic than Joyce's, his greater tendency to adopt splitting defences should not surprise us.

CHAPTER 3

PRODUCING DATA WITH DEFENDED SUBJECTS

We deliberately avoided saying anything in Chapter 2 about how we produced the data with Roger and Joyce that we went on to analyse in terms of their rather different, anxiety-driven investments. But, obviously, before data can be analysed they have first to be produced (or selected from an existing field); moreover, the quality of the analysis depends crucially on the quality of the data produced: 'rubbish in, rubbish out', as the saying goes. In this chapter we explore in detail the implications for data production of working with the premiss that all research subjects are meaning-making and defended subjects who:

- may not hear the question through the same meaning-frame as that of the interviewer or other interviewees;
- are invested in particular positions in discourses to protect vulnerable aspects of self;
- may not know why they experience or feel things in the way that they do;
- are motivated, largely unconsciously, to disguise the meaning of at least some of their feelings and actions.

Like many theoretical and methodological developments, we achieved our new insights through trial and error. Discovering what did not work spurred us on to try another method. In this chapter we shall take you through this story of trial and error, and the accompanying luck, that enabled us eventually to establish interview protocols for producing data with defended subjects. We start with our pilot attempts.

Mistaken attempts: our pilot studies

We produced, predictably, a number of draft interview schedules. The third of these was the one we decided to pilot as the first interview. It had a tripartite structure with each of the three sections devoted to one of our key theoretical themes (crime/victimisation, anxiety/worry and risk/safety). Because we were trying to tap into the particular history of individuals, questions were specific, asking after concrete incidents, or hypotheticals based on concrete incidents, wherever possible. These remained closely tied to our theoretical interests in discrepancies (between fear and risk, for example), with detailed alternative routes for 'yes' and 'no' answers (where applicable). The effort to remain close to an interviewee's own experiences was assisted by framing the questions along the lines of: 'What happened?', 'What did you do?', 'How did you feel?' Thus, we opened with a 'what' question ('What's the crime you most fear?') and checked whether it had happened to them. If it had, we followed up with 'What did you do?', 'How did you feel?' questions. Our wish to avoid generalisations led us also to ask our interviewees whether their feelings changed with the passage of time. Given our theoretical interest in intersubjective defences against anxiety, we also asked what any 'relevant others' did and felt each time. There were constant invitations to explain actions and feelings, motivated by our pursuit of contradictions, inconsistencies and the 'irrational' explanation. Thus, if the crime that interviewees feared most had not happened to them, they would be asked whether they felt it was likely to happen. A 'yes' response would be followed by 'Why do you think that?'; a 'no' answer by 'Why do you fear it?' Finally, in the attempt to be comprehensive we produced additional questions. In the section on fear of crime/victimisation, for example, we had questions relating to the crime 'you most fear' (see below for an example) and 'what (other) crime(s) you have most been a victim of', or might be, as well as questions about 'non-stranger' and violent crime (if not otherwise mentioned), and vigilantism.

Having completed the process of revising and refining questions through successive drafts, we were ready to try them out. The results were disappointing. Why this should be so started to become clear when we went through the resulting transcripts. What follows is an extract from one such transcript (broken down into three parts to make following it easier) and our critical evaluation of it. Graphically and somewhat embarrassingly, this evaluation illustrates the problems with what we, at this time, took to be a focused, concrete and hard-won approach.

Tony: What's the crime you most fear?
Ann: An offence against the person probably.
Tony: The person or your person?
Ann: Well, erm yes, I fear being hurt myself but I also fear for my children being hurt.
Tony: OK. Has, have you ever been hurt?
Ann: Yes.
Tony: And what did you do?
Ann: Can you be more specific, what do you mean?
Tony: Well, I mean you choose any incident that you can recall.
Ann: Where I've been physically hurt?
Tony: Where you've been physically hurt.

Although the opening question is an attempt to tap concretely into Ann's fear of crime, it seems to come across as abstract because it is introduced abruptly, devoid of context, and prior to the build-up of any rapport. The uncertain answer ('probably') matches the unwitting abstractness of the question. The interviewer then has to work to focus the answer ('The person or your person?'), to make it less abstract, echoing her words where possible ('have you ever been hurt?'). The result is a single word answer, 'yes'. The interviewer again tries to focus the respondent through a 'do' question ('And what did you do?'). This only succeeds in producing a request to the interviewer to be more specific. This is hardly surprising since no particular incident has yet been specified. In an attempt not to override her meaning-frame, the interviewer invites her to choose an incident, but this is still too general. Ann's subsequent request for clarification ('Where I've been physically hurt?') might be seen as an attempt to ask after the interviewer's meaning-frame, what the interviewer is really after. She probably does this because that is the kind of relationship that the question-and-answer approach has established; that is, the interviewer defines the agenda.

> Ann: Erm, it erm. Well, I've been hurt by people I've been in relationships with. Is that the sort of crime you're referring to?
> Tony: That's fine.
> Ann: It's varied what I've done. It depends on
> Tony: From what to what?
> Ann: Yes, it depends on what the circumstances were and whether I think I contributed to it or not, how I responded ultimately.
> Tony: So if you thought you contributed to it you did what?
> Ann: My usual response actually, if I describe my response, my response pattern to any situation where I've feel [*sic*] threatened, it'll probably help to answer the question. If I am threatened physically and it's not happened a lot but if I am I notice now that I have a patterned response which is, that I immediately go into shock and that it takes me a couple of days to recover from that actual physical shock and I, I experience the shock as though it were an accident or you know [*Tony*: Yes] my body closes down and I can't think about it and I just feel very numb and, erm, after a couple of days with not being able to think about it then my mind starts to process it and I start to analyse it. I've never ever called the police except on one occasion when my children were involved with my ex partner. So I've called the police on one occasion.
> Tony: But as well as going into shock are there other things you do?

Even when the interviewer agrees that an incident where Ann had been physically hurt was appropriate, she is still uncertain that being hurt by 'people I've been in relationships with' counts (for the interviewer). Reassurance on this score still leaves her unfocused since her responses have varied ('it depends'). Instead of getting her to focus on a particular incident, the interviewer picks up on this lead about her various responses. This effectively invites her to continue in a generalising mode ('it depends on ... the circumstances ... and whether I think

I contributed to it or not'). Perhaps realising the error, the interviewer attempts to recoup by specifying a 'contributory' situation: 'So if you thought you contributed to it you did what?' It is still too little; no actual incident has been specified so she plumps for her 'usual' (i.e. general) response, hoping this will help. The interviewer allows this and learns that usually she goes into shock, and on one occasion (and only one occasion) she called the police. This should have provided two openings: one towards her meaning-frame via a further exploration of the issue of 'shock'; the other (at last!) towards a specific incident: the time she called the police. The interviewer misses them both, clumsily cutting across her meaning-frame concerning shock in pursuit of an apparently concrete question: 'But … are there other things you do?'

> *Ann:* Well, I feel, do or feel?
> *Tony:* Do.
> *Ann:* It depends. If I'm able to access the person who's done it to me then I usually want to talk to them about it. Erm, but that's not always possible. What I've found is that when people hurt you they run away themselves and you're not able to actually resolve it and so therefore I think that exacerbates the shock I feel.
> *Tony:* Why?
> *Ann:* Because you're dealing with a range of feelings then [*Tony*: Right] which are not just about the physical assault.
> *Tony:* Can I just sort of be clear in my own mind what we're talking about here. You mentioned threat. Are we talking about threats of violence or actual violence?

At this point, Ann half re-introduces her meaning-frame ('Well, I feel', a reference back to her feelings of shock) before remembering the question specified 'things you do'. So she asks, 'do or feel?' Again, in the interest of (an apparent) concreteness, the interviewer reiterates 'do'. Once again she vacillates ('it depends'), and then generalises ('I usually want to talk to them about it … but that's not always possible … when people hurt you they run away'). The interviewer responds with a 'why' question, thus inviting further speculative theorising as to why someone running away 'exarcerbates the shock' she feels. Ann's answer ('Because you're dealing with a range of feelings then') makes sense but is still very general. In desperation, the interviewer seeks clarification as to 'what we're talking about here … Are we talking about threats of violence or actual violence?' Not only has any hint of a concrete incident disappeared, but the interviewer seems now to be completely adrift, not even knowing whether Ann is talking about 'threats' or 'actual violence'.

What happened? How did the interviewer's attempt to elicit concrete, detailed experiences manage to produce this vacillating, generalising account about what 'usually' happens? To answer this, it will be helpful to look at four approaches to interviewing and the different ways in which each would identify the problems in the above example. The four approaches are: traditional, feminist, narrative and clinical.

Traditional approaches

In traditional approaches, successful interviewing is seen as a matter of good technique. From this point of view we can examine the interviewer's mistakes, as we have done above; for example, the importance of starting with safe, unthreatening questions in the interests of developing rapport. However, though the somewhat abstract and abrupt opening was probably a mistake, we did not feel that it was decisive. Likewise, there were failures to follow up certain opportunities, such as Ann's 'shock' response to threatened violence, and the one time she called the police to deal with partner violence. Overall, though, we did not feel that we could place the blame at the door of either the interviewer or the respondent since the former was a sympathetic listener with a lot of professional experience and the latter was intelligent, thoughtful and articulate. The problem, we concluded, went deeper than a few mistakes, which all interviewers make – through tiredness, lapses of concentration, a clumsily worded question or tapping into unknown (and unknowable) sensitivities.

Feminist approaches

Feminist researchers have criticised unequal power relations in the interview, whether these are based on gender, race, class and/or something else (Stanley and Wise, 1983; Maynard and Purvis, 1994). This critique is part of a wider demand to counter the objectification of the interviewee which, it is argued, follows from the model of detached scientist making supposedly neutral enquiries through the interview. Both humanistic and feminist researchers have pursued this line of critique.[1] Feminists emphasise the way in which the subordination of women can be reproduced in the research relationship. Women's accounts can be constrained by the power of the interviewer and analysis taken out of their hands, thus producing outcomes against their interests. Consequently, feminists have stressed the importance of achieving symmetry in the social identities of the interview pair. In our example, it would probably be pointed out that a male interviewer, whom the female interviewee hardly knew, was inappropriate to the potential subject matter. It is possible that a woman interviewer, on this occasion, would have been better able to get Ann to talk concretely, in a less defended way, about her experiences of male violence[2]. In general, though not invariably, we went for same-sex interviewing for just this reason: to minimise the defensiveness brought on by sex differences. But power relations are more complex than the power differences based on sex, race, class or sexuality. For example, Currie and MacLean (1997) have evidence from the Islington Crime Survey to suggest that women disclose more sexual violence to male interviewers. If this is true generally, we could guess that some interviewees presume that women interviewers would be more judgemental and therefore prefer not to disclose domestic violence to them.[3]

Narrative approaches

The first two approaches remain within the framework of the traditional question-and-answer interview. Outside of this framework stand narrative (and usually clinical case-study) approaches, in which the researcher's responsibility is to be a good listener and the interviewee is a story-teller rather than a respondent. All structured interviews and most aspects of semi-structured interviews come under the question-and-answer type, where the interviewer sets the agenda and in principle remains in control of what information is produced. In this mode, the interviewer is imposing on the information in three ways: 'by selecting the theme and topics; by ordering the questions and by wording questions in his or her language' (Bauer, 1996: 2).

In the narrative approach, the agenda is open to development and change, depending on the narrator's experiences. At the pilot stage, we remained stuck in the conventional assumption of social-science research that the researcher asks questions. We could understand the problems in our example in terms of Mishler's (1986) argument that the question-and-answer method of interviewing has a tendency to suppress respondents' stories. It is not just a matter of being open to stories within the responses: we asked Ann to participate in a pilot interview because we knew she could tell stories about her experiences in the informal context in which Wendy knew her. By trying hard to comply with the interviewer's agenda, Ann was not able to convey her own relevant experiences. Chase (1995: 2) argues that 'attending to another's story in the interview context … requires an altered conception of what interviews are and how we should conduct them', a point to which we shall return in the next section.

According to Polanyi, the difference between a story and a report (of the kind that is often elicited in the traditional research interview) is that, in telling a story, the narrator takes responsibility for 'making the relevance of the telling clear' (quoted in Chase, 1995: 2). This approach therefore emphasises the meaning that is created within the research pair. It also recognises that the story told is constructed (within the research and interview context) rather than being a neutral account of a pre-existing reality. Stories have conventional structures which are arranged to provide coherence and causal sequence ('so then'); they have a beginning, a middle and an end.[4] According to some, however, the narrative form has an even more central place in human life: 'there does not exist, and never has existed, a people without narratives' (Barthes, cited in Polkinghorne, 1988: 14); narrative is 'the primary form by which human experience is made meaningful ... it organises human experiences into temporally meaningful episodes' (Polkinghorne, 1988: 1); 'thinking, perception, imagination and moral decision-making are based on narrative structure' (Sarbin, cited in Josselson, 1992: 155). More recently, self-identity has been seen as being achieved by narratives of the self (Day Sclater, 1998).

Claims for the efficacy and appropriateness of a narrative method for studying experiences and meaning in context (Mishler, 1986; Josselson, 1992; Riessman, 1993) have been subject to the basic problems of any other hermeneutic approach. What is the relation of a story to the events to which it refers (or, as we labelled it earlier, the relation of word to world)? How is truth compromised by the story-teller's motivations and memory? Since one of the defining features of the narrative form is coherence (Linde, 1993; Rosenthal, 1993), how does this affect our knowledge of the potential incoherence of life as it is lived? In the language of social science, these are questions about the reliability and validity of eliciting narratives as a research method. Some narrative researchers (for example, Bauer, 1996) have set aside these questions by taking the position that the object of narrative analysis is the narrative itself, as opposed to the events being narrated or the experiences or character of the narrator. This was not so for us when we turned to a narrative method. The focus of our analysis is the people who tell us stories about their lives: the stories themselves are a means to understand our subjects better. While stories are obviously not providing a transparent account through which we learn truths, story-telling stays closer to actual life-events than methods that elicit explanations. According to Bauer (1996: 3), 'narrations are rich in indexical statements' (by 'indexical' he means that 'reference is made to concrete events in place and time').

Clinical case-study approaches

One response to the perception that survey-type research was losing sight of an understanding of whole people in real-life contexts was to look outside research to practitioners for models of social knowledge. Clinicians work primarily with case studies and the psychoanalytic interview is a useful model for qualitative research in numerous respects

(Kvale, 1999). Psychoanalysts have a model of knowledge which places primary responsibility on their own involvement in understanding a patient. According to Berg and Smith, 'the complex emotional and intellectual forces that influence the conduct of our inquiry … are at once the source of our insight and our folly' (1988: 11). As researchers, therefore, we cannot be detached but must examine our subjective involvement because it will help to shape the way in which we interpret the interview data. This approach is consistent with the emphasis on reflexivity in the interview, but it understands the subjectivity of the interviewer through a model which includes unconscious, conflictual forces rather than simply conscious ones:

> the process of self-scrutiny is central to our definition of clinical research because it can yield information about the intellectual and emotional factors that inevitably influence the researcher's involvement and activity, and at the same time provide information about the dynamics of the individual or social system being studied. The self-scrutiny process is difficult and complex precisely because both researcher and the 'researched' are simultaneously influencing each other. Since this is occurring in ways that initially are out of the awareness of the parties involved, scrutiny is an absolutely necessary part of social science research. (Berg and Smith, 1988: 31; see also Devereux, 1967)

In recognising the importance of unconscious dynamics in the research interview, this approach also notices the defences against anxiety. Part of the problem in our example could have been the anxiety of the interviewer. This may have resulted from a combination of the unfamiliarity of the (first-time) situation and developing worries about the success of the interview after high expectations of it. More tellingly, what the interviewer had stumbled upon was the hornet's nest of Ann's painful experiences of partner violence. Positing a defended subject enabled us to see that part of Ann's vacillation was probably a largely unconscious sounding out of the interviewer, staying safe through comfortable, well-rehearsed generalisations. Utilising the concept of the defended subject enabled us also to interpret Ann's responses as established defences working to protect her from her own painful experiences of domestic violence (which we knew about prior to the interview). According to this approach, her well-rehearsed generalisations about what she does in this situation and what she does in that, intelligent and articulate though they are, are part of a defensive strategy, a strategy of intellectualising, of 'managing' painfully confusing emotional experiences through words which offer (apparently) the comfort of comprehension and the prospect of control. Although we only have evidence of Ann's defensive strategy in this particular, relational, setting of the research interview, it was enough to convince us of the need to find an approach which took account of such defences.

The biographical-interpretative method

At this point, somewhat fortuitously, we stumbled across the biographical-interpretative method, first developed by German sociologists producing accounts of the lives of holocaust survivors and Nazi soldiers (Rosenthal and Bar-On, 1992; Schutze, 1992; Rosenthal, 1993). The biographical-interpretative method is part of the narrative tradition in social-science research, a tradition which has been most developed in life-story research (see, for example, Plummer, 1995).

However, given our understanding of the way in which unconscious defences affect the information that is produced in the research relationship and the way in which it is interpreted, we wanted to incorporate this idea of the defended subject into our use of a narrative method. Schutze's (1992) article, an example of the biographical-interpretative tradition, revealed that elicited accounts such as those of Nazi soldiers will be highly defensive ones, given the painful subject matter, which needed a methodological strategy to uncover what he calls 'faded-out memories and delayed recollections of emotionally or morally disturbing war experiences' (Schutze, 1992: 347). Although Schutze sees 'some intersections between Freud's impressive theory on repression' (1992: 359, n1) and his own method, this insight is not developed. The main theoretical principle is not the defended subject, but the idea that there is a *Gestalt* (a whole which is more than the sum of its parts, an order or hidden agenda) informing each person's life which it is the job of biographers to elicit intact, and not destroy through following their own concerns (Rosenthal, 1990). The German biographers' strategy for eliciting narratives – which we adopted and adapted – can be summarised in terms of four principles, each designed to facilitate the production of the interviewee's meaning-frame or *Gestalt*, as follows.

Use open-ended not closed questions, the more open the better

'How safe do you feel walking alone in this area after dark?', with respondents expected to tick one of four categories on a Likert scale, is, as we saw in Chapter 1, a completely closed question. Our opening question to Ann, 'What's the crime you most fear?', is open, but in a narrow way, which may help account for its failure to elicit much from her. In linking fear with crime, it reveals what sort of fear interests the interviewer, but, in so doing, it may work to suppress the meaning of fear to Ann, which may have no apparent connection to crime. To learn about the meaning of fear to Ann, a more open question, such as 'What do you most fear?', would be necessary. The presumption of the biographical method is that it is only in this way, by tracking Ann's fears through her meaning-frames, that we are likely to discover the 'real' meaning of fear of crime to her – how it relates to her life.

Elicit stories

Eliciting stories has the virtue of indexicality, of anchoring people's accounts to events that have actually happened. To that extent such accounts have to engage with reality, even while compromising it in the service of self-protection. Eliciting stories from people is not always a simple matter, especially from those who feel their lives lack suffi-cient interest or worth to justify 'a story'. And, no doubt for a variety of different reasons, people's story-telling ability varies enormously. However, given the importance of the narrative form to all social com-munication, a story is often chosen to answer even direct questions, especially when interviewees are uncertain what is required. It's a 'Well, this is the story of my relationship to your chosen topic, you decide whether it's what you're after' sort of reply. The particular story told, the manner and detail of its telling, the points emphasised, the morals drawn, all represent choices made by the story-teller. Such choices are revealing, often more so than the teller suspects. This char-acteristic of story-telling – to contain significances beyond the teller's intentions – is what it shares with the psychoanalytic method of free associations. The implications of this for the traditional interview method are a recommendation to 'narrativise topics', that is, to turn questions about given topics into story-telling invitations. In this light, the open-ended 'What do you most fear?', which could elicit a one-word answer rather than a story, would be modified to read 'Tell me about your experiences of fear' or, better, because more specific, 'Tell me about a time when you were fearful.'

Avoid 'why' questions

With Ann (above), we saw that a why question elicited an intellectual-isation. While this was appropriate to the question, it was uninforma-tive in terms of the research questions. At first glance this is the most surprising principle since it is counter-intuitive: surely people's own explanations of their actions or feelings are useful routes to under-standing them? Indeed, researchers sometimes assume that they can simply translate their research question into the question for intervie-wees. Sacks, for example, found that because she asked sociological questions her women interviewees offered sociological responses, but 'the abstraction of such talk – its disconnection from their actual lives, made it hollow' (cited in Chase, 1995: 4). She concluded that it was a mistake to ask those kinds of question. However, as we argued in Chapter 1, people could only be their own best explainers if they conformed to the model of the rational, information-processing subject of psychology. This is not the case, as we saw with Roger. His own account of why he was fearful of crime spoke of contemporary tales of murder and mayhem, despite evidence of the mundane reality of local crime, and compared these with the 'golden age' of his disciplined childhood, despite evidence of a brutally cruel father. Moreover, so common is this talk of the breakdown of law and order in everday life that it becomes all things to all people and therefore empty of concrete meaning. It was only when, via Roger's stories, we could get behind this empty, cliché-ridden discursive front to the defensive investments it concealed that we were able to unpack the meaning to Roger of fear of crime, namely, its connection with his loss of patriarchal authority.

Follow up using respondents' ordering and phrasing

This involves attentive listening and possibly some note-taking during the initial narration in order to be able to follow up themes in their narrated order. In doing this, the respondent's own words and phrases should be used in order to respect and retain the interviewee's meaning-frames. As always, the follow-up questions constructed should be as open as possible and framed so as to elicit further narratives.

For the German biographers, the method entails a single, open, initial question which is also an invitation: 'Please, tell me your life story' (Rosenthal, 1990).[5] We are not biographers or life-story researchers and have adapted the questions in this light. Our interest in specific events has been labelled as 'focused interviews' by Mishler (1986: 99). In both cases, the art and skill of the exercise is to assist narrators to say more about their lives (to assist the emergence of *Gestalts*) without at the same time offering interpretations, judgements or otherwise imposing the interviewer's own relevancies, which would thus destroy the interviewee's *Gestalt*. Apparently simple, it required discipline and practice to transform ourselves from the highly visible asker of our questions to the almost invisible, facilitating catalyst to their stories. Being 'almost invisible' does not imply a belief in an objective interviewer who has no effects on the production of accounts, a point we return to below. It means not imposing a structure on the narrative.

The importance of free association

This is not the place to explore fully the interesting question of the relationship between the German sociologist biographers' understanding of *Gestalt* and our psychoanalytically derived understanding of anxiety (see Hollway and Jefferson, 1997). What we would like to draw attention to are the similarities between the principle of respecting the narrator's *Gestalt* and the psychoanalytic method of free association. By asking the patient to say whatever comes to mind, the psychoanalyst is eliciting the kind of narrative that is not structured according to conscious logic, but according to unconscious logic; that is, the associations follow pathways defined by emotional motivations, rather than rational intentions. According to psychoanalysis, unconscious dynamics are a product of attempts to avoid or master anxiety.[6] This suggests that anxieties and attempts to defend against them, including the identity investments these give rise to, provide the key to a person's *Gestalt*. By eliciting a narrative structured according to the principles of free association, therefore, we secure access to a person's concerns which would probably not be visible using a more traditional method. While a common concern of both approaches is to elicit detail, narrative analysis has a preoccupation with coherence which we do not share. Free associations defy narrative conventions and enable the analyst to pick up on incoherences (for example, contradictions, elisions, avoidances) and accord them due significance.

Narrative questions in the first interview

Following our attendance at a biographical-interpretative method workshop, we set about revising our interview schedule. We considered asking one single question (as the German biographers do), but our three-part theoretical structure – crime/victimisation, risk/safety, anxiety/worry – imposed by the fact that we were researching specifically into the fear of crime, seemed to provide an important frame for eliciting what we wanted to know. Life stories can be structured by an infinite number of themes, but our research provided a particular frame that we could not ignore. We decided, therefore, upon six questions deriving from our theoretical structure and a seventh about moving into the area (see Box 3.1). Each question was followed up in terms of detail and time periods, following the order of the narrative.

Box 3.1   First Interview Questions

1   Can you tell me about how crime has impacted on your life since you've been living here?
2   Can you tell me about unsafe situations in your life since you've been living here?

---

3   Can you think of something that you've read, seen or heard about recently that makes you fearful? Anything [not necessarily about crime].
4   Can you tell me about risky situations in your life since you've been living here?
5   Can you tell me about times in your life recently when you've been anxious?
6   Can you tell me about earlier times in your life when you've been anxious?
7   Can you tell me what it was like moving to this area?

It can be argued that, by asking the questions we ask, notably by asking about anxiety, we produce the anxiety that we are seeking to establish empirically. Of course, all research in a sense produces its answers by the very frame through which the questions are set. No frame is ever neutral, and neither was ours. However, as the answers of our interviewees made clear, the diversity of the stories elicited demonstrated that their accounts were not constructed by them. This, we feel, is related to our central idea that people's lives have a bio-graphically unique 'reality' which our open questions were designed to elicit. Only if this were not the case could it be argued that the answers given by respondents are merely 'produced' by the discursive frame of the questions.

Question 1 aims to elicit any associations to crime. We worded it in this way so that it did not assume victimisation, and indeed it elicited stories about criminal involvement from several young men. Usually it provided an account of criminal victimisations directly to the respondent and of crimes happening locally. Though it did often elicit stories as it was intended to, we now consider this question to be insufficiently narrativised since it invites respondents to talk about the general 'impact of crime' on their life over, in some cases, a very long period ('since you've been living here'). The best questions require the inter-viewee to be specific about times and situations; thus, a better question would have been 'Can you tell me about times when crime has impacted on your life since you've been living here?' Further questions to the main question follow the principle of respecting the respondent's meaning-frames, remaining faithful to the order and wording in which they presented their associations (see below for a detailed example). Questions 2 and 4 aim to elicit stories relating to safety and risk respec-tively, providing us with two routes to the same theoretical point. Safety is the same concept as that used in the British Crime Survey question ('How safe do you feel ...?'), but in the way we framed this question we did not assume fear. While the notion of being 'at risk' is similar, we wanted to broaden out the question so as not to talk specifically about the risk of criminal victimisation. We also wished to leave open the issue of whether a respondent associated to being at risk or to being a risk-taker. Question 3 is designed to explore some links between the fear of crime and discourses available in the media. Questions 5 and 6 are both about anxiety. These are separated into recent and past anxiety in recognition of the importance, according to psychoanalytic theory, of childhood trauma in producing adult fears and chronic anxiety. Question 7 was added in order to take into account the fact that a person's perception of a neighbourhood will be influenced by comparing it with where they lived previously. This question asked for stories about moving in order to elicit such comparisons. It was also likely to be a neutral question with which to end.

The questions did not always elicit different stories. However, the different frames of the questions meant that people could elaborate different associations to the same memory. After the first question we were not asking specifically about crime, although the overall frame in which the research interview was presented defined crime as a key theme. In question 3, we widened the frame specifically by asking about any media stimulus that had made people fearful, giving respondents explicit permission to broaden out. This was informed by our hypothesis that generalised anxiety might become invested in, and be expressed by, fear of crime, or it might be expressed in other concerns, for example environmental pollution. Any associations to the question were therefore encouraged and legitimately within our interests.

Developing our free-association narrative interview

How did our new, story-based approach fare when put to the test? In this section we try to show something of its strengths: first, in showing how free associations in the narrative revealed significant personal meanings which were not necessarily obvious at the time; secondly, in securing an unexpected admission which enforced a re-evaluation of our interviewee.

An emergent Gestalt

In what follows, we use the transcript of the beginning of the first interview with Jane, a 19-year-old white woman, single mother of two children, aged two and three, living on a high-crime council housing estate.[7] (The interviewer's question was a version of question 1, above, so this excerpt was at the very beginning of the taped interview.)

> *Wendy:*   Tell me first of all how crime has had any effects on you since you moved here.

> *Jane:*   Em, it's just you know, like, we got broken into once. But they didn't seem to take owt. They just took stuff outside there, and that were it. They must er, I must 'ave come 'ome and they were 'ere [1]. And just – I see police, y'know, bringing cars up from fields at back [2]. There's always motor bikes. Kids on motor bikes [3]. They just don't seem to do nowt [4]. They just see 'em go past and – it's just like – you know things like – there's a 'ouse up there and some kids 'ave broken into it. It were like in daylight. Kicking door down and smashing window – nobody were doing nowt [5]. There was somebody living next door, people across road, nobody seemed to do owt [6]. And they're all their kids. And it's like – they just let the kids do what they want. They don't bother [7]. [*Wendy*: Right]. There're like, there's like one and two-year-olds just play-ing out on the street and it's all that kind of thing [8].

At first sight, the interview looks far from promising. It is not always clear what Jane is referring to and she dries up quite quickly. This excerpt does not have the coherence or conventional structure of a story. The interviewer's technique involves not intervening until the interchange is handed back and identifying the themes which are apparent, so as to return to them in the order of their appearance to elicit further detail. Eight themes were identifiable in this short extract. Jane mentions the break-in, summed up in four short sentences [1]. Her next association [2] is to the police in the context of a different crime: police retrieving stolen cars from where they have been dumped. This leads her [3] to think of another instance of local joy-riding: kids on motor bikes. Her theme is still the police [4] (though she does not specify this here, the interviewer does not intervene to clarify): the police go past, but 'don't seem to do nowt'. In mid-sentence Jane shifts to a different example of inactivity [5], in this instance where 'nobody were doing nowt', even though kids had broken into a house and were vandalising it. She elaborates on the nobody [6], instancing neigh-bours' inactivity in the face of kids breaking the law. Her train of asso-ciation is then [7] to parents who do not stop these activities and finally [8] to parents' more general negligence as instanced by very young children playing out unsupervised.

Because this pathway of associations is produced out of Jane's con-cerns, the hypothesis is that the whole will signify more than the sum of the parts (this is definitional of a *Gestalt*). A quick-witted interviewer, who has already taken biographical details, may have realised the sig-nificance of where this young woman ended her first contribution. Certainly, as the interview developed, there were numerous pointers to the fact that Jane's relation to the council estate where she had lived for 12 months was informed more than anything else by her concern for how she was going to bring up her two young boys in this context of precocious delinquency. Her disapproval of the negligence of some parents on the estate was an expression of her difference in this respect ('I couldn't believe it, me', 'Mum couldn't believe it'), on which were pinned, presumably, her hopes that her children would not go the same way. This was all the more important given that she and her family represented one of the stereotypes of the negligent mother: a young, single, white parent, with mixed-race children. This key to her *Gestalt* manifested itself at the first opportunity, that is, at the end of her first unimpeded response to a question framed for maximum openness.[8] It had actually entailed her going 'off' the question, in the sense that she had started by listing some crimes and then moved on to other, non-criminal, issues which for her were intimately associated, but of greater concern. It is her emotional concerns which produce this pathway of associations. She eventually mentioned this core concern, namely, the difficulty of bringing up children in such a delinquency-prone environment, later in the first interview: 'It's just with these [her children] getting older. It's like everybody round 'ere, I mean they're – dunno – it's attitudes and that.' To have confined the interview to crime would have been to rule out this, her central preoccupation. In so doing, it would have risked misunderstanding the meaning of crime and fear of crime in her life.

An open question and an unusual admission

The following extract is taken from the transcript of our first interview with Tommy (whom we meet again in Chapter 4), a 42-year-old white man from a large local family who has lived on the same high-crime estate for 33 years, currently with his common-law wife, their 5-year-old son and her two older sons.

Tony: So you started there by talking about the two times in your life when you've been ill and that made you anxious. Er, has there been any other times when you've felt anxious about anything? Or is it just about health?

Tommy: Well, actually I were frightened when I lost me dad.

Tony: Yeah?

Tommy: Yeah. Only one in family who were frightened, 'cos we 'ad 'im at 'ome.

Tony: Yeah. Tell me about it.

Tommy: Well, he worked all 'is life, me dad. Never got – and 'e was 65 and not even got 'is bus pass. And it *really* 'urt me that. That er, 'e died in pain in 'ospital as well. They fetched 'im … home. Fetched 'im over, put 'im at side of wall and they took lid off. You know what I mean? Me dad were laid there and everybody, when we come down next morning, oh I couldn't go to sleep that night thinking about it. And everybody come down stairs, 'oh God bless', all mourners, everybody came – 'cos 'e were well loved me dad. They loved me dad on estate. And everybody kissed 'im bar me because I were frightened. Eventually we cremated 'im and I went back to work week after and I broke down at work. Because I didn't do what I should have done. I broke down at work, they fetched me 'ome from work and I were off work three week.

Tony: Three weeks?

Tommy: I broke down, aye. I went to bed one night and I'll never forget it happened. Me mam will probably tell ya as well, when you go and see 'er.[9] Went to bed one night, summat woke me up. I woke up and I looked at bottom end of bed. Me dad were there. Me dad turned round 'don't worry about it, I still love ya.' Just disappeared. Got up next morning, I told me mother. 'Oh you 'aven't 'ave ya?' I said 'aye' I says 'he says he loved me and told me not to worry about it, because I didn't kiss 'im'. I wish I 'ad 'ave done na 'cos it's 20 year na since we lost 'im.

The interviewer starts by picking up on Tommy's previous answer concerning anxiety, attempting to elicit other times in his life when he has felt anxious. This 'time-based' approach is a good example of open questioning, as is the addition 'about anything', but it is not an invitation to generalise. His response ('I were frightened when I lost me dad') uses the vocabulary of fear, not anxiety. Rather than seek to clarify and risk cutting across his meaning-frame, the interviewer 'invites' him to continue with a non-committal but interested 'yeah?'. Tommy starts to tell the story and is explicitly encouraged to continue. Note the absence of any attempt by the interviewer to check the story's relevance (to the project) in advance. What follows is a richly thematised story of what his dad's death meant to him: the injustice of a working man dying before enjoying any of the fruits of retirement ('not even got 'is bus pass'); his inability to sleep with the dead body in the house; pride in his dad's reputation ('They loved me dad on estate'); and, finally, the revelation (and the 'anxious' point of the story) of his fearful inability to kiss his dead dad, to do what he 'should have done', and his subsequent breakdown at work. Given the richness of this story, the interviewer might have been tempted to follow up the themes it revealed (hopefully respecting Tommy's ordering). But it is important to ensure that each story is finished uninterrupted. Hence, the interviewer merely echoes, in questioning fashion, Tommy's endpoint 'Three weeks?', thereby implicitly inviting him to continue should he wish. The reward for this disciplined reticence is another extraordinary revelation, this time about a comforting visitation by his father's ghost.

It is unlikely that this story would have come out using our old schedule: first, because there was no specific question inviting it; secondly, because an interventionist ethos probably would have 'interrupted' Tommy before he got this far back in his associations. What new understanding did this story make possible? We approached this question through the surprise the admission engendered in the interviewer. This surprise had partly to do with the unusual nature of the story itself. But it had mostly to do with the way in which it appeared to contradict the cheerful, confident and not obviously fearful Tommy which had been revealed through his other recounted stories. Something previously unknown (and unsuspected) had now been revealed: that Tommy as a young man had experienced extreme and distressing anxiety. Without attempting to assess the story's ultimate significance, a task which would require a knowledge of Tommy beyond the remit of this chapter,[10] it is clear that such memories have significance and have to be accounted for. Any assessment of Tommy after this had to make sense of both the cheery confidence and this new evidence of some underlying anxiety. Gradually, we saw the contrasts in Tommy's account as part of a pattern in which unpalatable realities were idealistically glossed, a pattern which revealed important clues about his characteristic structure of defences (see Chapter 4). Though we might have got there without this story, its dramatic impact was such as to ensure that we had to question appearances more searchingly than we might otherwise have done. Tommy's story is an example of how a narrative elicited by our method, while fashioned as a story and probably told many times, retains its anchor in a real event in Tommy's life: his breakdown after his dad's death.

The second interview

Since our theoretical starting-point neither takes respondents' accounts at face value nor expects them to be able to understand completely their own actions, motivations or feelings, we decided early on to have a double interview. The first interview would enable us to establish a preliminary symptomatic reading: to interrogate critically what was said, to pick up the contradictions, inconsistencies, avoidances and changes of emotional tone. The second interview would act as a check in various ways by allowing us to seek further evidence to test our emergent hunches and provisional hypotheses (see Hollway and Jefferson, 1997). It also gave interviewees a chance to reflect.

The second interview was fixed, if possible, one week after the first. In between times, we two researchers listened to each tape together: those we had conducted ourselves and those conducted by the other. In this way, we tried to triangulate, to get both an insider and an outsider perspective on the interview. There would typically be many pauses in the playback while the significance of a part of the narrative was discussed and we attempted to get a reading of the person which was sensitive to all the details offered and did not iron out the contradictions in his or her accounts. From notes taken during this process, the interviewer constructed a series of tailor-made narrative questions for the second interview. Often these were based on issues which appeared to be symptomatic of tension or conflict in an account, as in contradictions, avoidances or hesitations. It also meant that we gave ourselves permission to explore themes that may have been significant through their absence, rather than remaining within the confines of the account we had been given; for example, if no mention has been made of a person's childhood and parents. Often, though, it was a question of asking for further stories to illustrate themes that had already arisen. For example, Jane had said little about her parents, though it was evident that they had been very supportive on most occasions. She had mentioned a time when she had had no contact with them, as a result of sticking by her partner, whom they knew was violent to their daughter. The question constructed to elicit narrrative on this topic, while remaining as open as possible, was 'What happened that led up to your falling out with your parents?'

After this second set of narrative questions, we went through a set of structured questions with each participant, if answers had not already been covered previously. Since the narrative interview format does not guarantee systematic coverage of issues, we judged this information necessary to enable comparisons across demographic groups and different localities, in our case high- and low-crime council housing estates.

The overall effect of this method was that, in the vast majority of cases, interviewees warmed to the whole event, and to the interviewer, because they had an experience of being paid attention to and taken seriously through their own, self-styled account. In Jane's case, after the tape was turned off at the end she commented that she had told the interviewer more (notably about the traumatic relationship with her ex-partner) than anyone except her mum. This reflects the gradual build-up of trust over two interviews. (We explore this process in detail below.) In this regard the second interview is significant in that it feels like resuming an established relationship rather than starting out as strangers, as in the first. Interviewees' preparedness to open out intimate material also reflects the building up of an expectation that stories are what the researcher wants – that they are interesting, relevant and valued. This expectation has to be actively built because the normal expectation is otherwise; that is, that an interviewer will come round with a batch of questions, for which one-word or short replies are required. Our overall impression was that most people liked telling stories – even about discomforting events – once they felt reasonably trusting of the framework and relationship within which these were being received.

Intersubjectivity and the research relationship

Up until now, we have focused on the interviewee, with the role of the interviewer confined largely to that of eliciting narratives. This is not the whole truth since the resulting narratives are always a product of the relationship between interviewer and interviewee. Here we explore the dynamics of the interview pair and their importance for the production of data. Where appropriate the voice of the author changes to 'I' (Wendy) rather than 'we' since the example involved Wendy Hollway's research encounter with Jane (whom you have met earlier in this chapter).

The piece of evidence we wish to explore is the following, from my field notes following the second (last) interview with Jane: 'I am having difficulty disconnecting; wondering if I should have stayed and talked; feeling that it ended abruptly.' We chose the interview with Jane for two reasons. First, it was one which did not go smoothly according to the principles that we have set out above. This may help to explore the processes involved, which might otherwise be less visible. Secondly, I was left with very strong feelings in relation to Jane, feelings that were not typical of most of my research relationships, and it is this phenomenon that I want to use to understand the dynamics of the research relationship. As Walkerdine puts it, '[the fact] that the feelings came up in me told me something ... that I wanted to take as data' (1997: 67).

In line with our theoretical starting-point, we intend to construe both researcher and researched as anxious, defended subjects, whose mental boundaries are porous where unconscious material is concerned. This means that both will be subject to projections and introjections of ideas and feelings coming from the other person. It also means that the impressions that we have about each other are not derived simply from the 'real' relationship, but that what we say and do in the interaction will be mediated by internal fantasies which derive from our histories of significant relationships. Such histories are often accessible only through our feelings and not through our conscious awareness. If we start from these theoretical principles, it follows that the information of our feelings in and around the interview are of value for understanding the dynamics of the research relationship. Therefore they are important to how the data are produced.

Walkerdine (1997) uses examples from her fieldwork observations in families to argue for the importance of being aware of the researcher's feelings that are brought up in the interview (and, subsequently, when analysing it):

> [The researcher's feelings] tell us about how a researcher comes to produce such an account and opens it to the possibility of different readings of the same material. It tells us that the process of reading itself is not all in the text, but is produced out of a complex interaction between reader and text. But perhaps it tells us more than this: as a researcher, I am no more, no different from the subjects of my research. (Walkerdine, 1997: 73)

In Chapter 2, the concept of unconscious intersubjectivity was applied in order to understand our interviewees in their daily relationships with others. If that proposition has any validity, it must be extended to apply to the relationship which is created in order to carry out the research.

Researchers do not usually regard it as important to record their feelings and fantasies in their field notes (though psychoanalysts do so in their clinical notes precisely because of the theoretical model that they use). Going back to the information recorded about Jane in my field notes, I wish there was a more thorough record of my impressions. None the less, I will examine the entry with which I started this section as an example of the complexity of the dynamics that were set up between Jane and me in the space of only two interviews, one week apart, each of which lasted for a little over an hour. I have re-read the transcripts, which go some way to immerse me back into the atmosphere of the interview. Being aware of the gaps in my memory after several years, I have also gone back to the audiotapes. There, the tone of our interchanges and its variations are much more evident. It serves as a reminder, too, of the context of our interview: both Jane's young children were present at both interviews (though the younger was asleep throughout the first one). There were constant interruptions as Jane attempted to keep them occupied and I tried not to ignore their presence.

First impressions

First impressions contain much that eludes our conscious assessment of another person. Moreover, these feelings continue in the relationship. We both (Wendy and Tony) knocked on Jane's door to ask if she would be willing to talk about crime on the estate, her experiences of it and her worries.[11] She took a long time to answer the door and we noted that she seemed nervous and embarrassed, perhaps depressed. She was pale and her hands were covered in eczema. She told us that there was 'only' her living there (and her two boys), as if she didn't qualify as a household. Our immediate response was to feel sorry for her situation. She agreed to take part and I fixed up two interviews with her. In the event she forgot both of these, though I had written them down for her. At the second interview she was still in her pyjamas, although it was midday.

It is relevant to imagine how Jane must have seen us: a couple of well-spoken researchers from the university.[12] We know from the interviews how important education was to her as a way of escaping her current situation (she had done well at school, taking her GCSEs while six months' pregnant, but then left and had to give up college when she gave birth to the second child). It seems likely, therefore, that we signified all the advantages of an interesting, well-paid job which comes with education. After the tape-recorder was turned off following the second interview, she asked me what I did for my job.

As on this occasion, we usually chose to interview our own sex (but not always – each case was considered individually against a range of factors of which sex was only one). Jane and I were both white – relevant for talk on race arising from Jane talking about having mixed-race children. Our class difference was stark and this probably signified through the educational difference. Finally, I was probably close to the age of Jane's mother. I think it was this structural feature of our identities which precipitated the unconscious dynamics of which I got a glimpse in my unease about leaving Jane at the end of the second interview.

My contention is that unconsciously I positioned Jane as 'daughter' and she positioned me as 'mother' (I put these in inverted commas because they are not meant literally but refer to the transferences of parts of the original mother–daughter relationship to the new relationship). There is considerable psychoanalytic work to suggest that parent–child relations are unconsciously transferred into other, daily social relations. Roper (1996), for example, has argued that there are influential unconscious dynamics in organisational structures which often mimic the power and other emotional dynamics of family relations. This dimension has been theorised through the experiences of psychoanalysts using the concepts of transference and countertransference (see Hinshelwood, 1991). Transference refers to the unconscious transferring of other emotionally significant relationships on to the therapist by the patient; countertransference to the therapist's responses to these transferences, as well as their own transferring of emotionally significant relationships on to the patient. In what follows we will try to convey the intersubjective quality of the interview and its changes. We want to show how the data are co-produced out of some subtle and largely unconscious dynamics.

Unconscious dynamics and the co-production of data

Jane's talk was halting and it was rare that she got into telling a story without trailing off. She often referred to things indirectly in ways that were not clear. It is perhaps not relevant to ask whether she was like this in other settings; the fact is that, faced with me, an articulate interviewer, she was fairly inarticulate. It could well have been an effect of her worries about talking to a stranger at all, although from the beginning she seemed pleased to be involved (she had very little adult company and often felt lonely) and came across as quite friendly. My response was actively to intervene in the account to encourage her to say more, to follow through, to give examples. The transcript does not remotely resemble the ideal of a narrative interview when, having asked the question, the researcher should shut up and engage in good listening. It is not that I was always interrupting (though I did, despite myself). Rather, when Jane trailed off, I felt responsible for keeping the interview going. This became self-fulfilling as our interchange developed a predictable pattern. However, I managed increasingly to ask for, and elicit, stories, as she came to realise that this was what I wanted. Further changes became apparent in the second interview. This was characterised by a lot more fluent interchange between us and parts where my interventions were more of the 'mmm', 'yeah' and 'can you say more' type.

None of these types of intervention are neutral or can ever be neutral. That goal is a hangover from beliefs about scientific objectivity. The question, we believe, is this: can the researcher's interventions be positive and produce the kind of understanding that will enhance trust? This is instrumental (it will improve rapport and enhance what may be told), but it can also be beneficial, rather than exploitative, for the interviewee. There are two examples from early in the first interview when my interventions could be understood as imposing my meanings on Jane: when I positioned her 'as a mother' and 'different' from other mothers on the estate:

> *Jane:*   It's just with these getting older. It's like everybody round 'ere. I mean they're – dunno – it's attitudes and that – they're all, it's like the [*Wendy*: Is it for the kids?] kids' language and everything. You 'ear mothers and that shouting and swearing and everything along there. I'm like, couldn't believe it.
>
> *Wendy:*   So you don't – as a mother – you
>
> *Jane:*   Yeah, it's just these growing up round 'ere.
>
> *Wendy:*   You feel as if you're different from the ones you hear?
>
> *Jane:*   Yeah. I don't know that I'd like to say different, it's just their attitudes. You know what I mean. They just seem, seem to let the kids just

However, I would like to suggest another interpretation to that of me imposing my meanings on Jane (the two may not be mutually exclusive). It is likely that her tendency not to finish her sentences (not to secure what she means in words) is about her emotional difficulties with the ideas that she is expressing. I think I was trying to put into words what she was conveying to me; namely, her concerns as a mother who felt different from the mothers she saw around her (whom later on she called 'rough'). When I suggested 'you're different' and she disagreed, she was being careful not to be seen to set herself above the mothers she was talking about. Her experiences of moving in suggested that they would probably have positioned her as bottom of the pile: maybe she feared I would too. At the same time, the way she was mothering her boys felt different to her.

Recognition and containment

Some contemporary psychoanalysts conceptualise aspects of unconscious intersubjectivity in the concepts of recognition and containment,[13] which are useful in understanding what it is in the research (or other) relationship which helps trust to develop. We will illustrate the meaning and utility of both concepts through the next example.

A significant portion of the second interview concerned Jane's accounts of the violence to her of the children's father. These included his jealousy, her attempts to leave, his threats and – the moment after which there was no going back – the time when he hit her when she had the new baby in her arms. The tenor of a lot of her accounts was quite emotionally flat: she reiterated often in the interview things like 'It didn't seem so bad at the time.' Not surprisingly after her horrendous experiences, it was difficult to feel just how bad it had been. This kind of information is sufficiently shocking that it is easy for the listener to defend against it, for example by moving on to the next question, or attempting to represent it as less nasty than it sounded. My comment when she told me that she had a scar on her leg from his knife (which he always carried) was 'It must have been petrifying.' Jane's response this time was not to make light of it, but to tell me a detail which she had left out, perhaps because it was too frightening to remember; she answered 'It were, cos 'e were threatening it me to me throat.' My phrases were often ones which tried to reflect the 'reality' of her emotional experience, even if it was hidden behind her defences. Soon after, picking up her word 'depressed', I commented:

> *Wendy:* Mmm. Quite enough to make anyone depressed.
> *Jane:* I did – did think. I just wanted to go and die, do you know what I mean? I just …
> *Wendy:* Did you think about dying?
> *Jane:* Yeah. Just – I didn't do owt like. I just really thought I'm gonna [*pause*] or I wanted 'im to die really.
> *Wendy:* Were you tempted to use that knife on him?
> *Jane:* Yeah, I were tempted really. And I thought, I knew I'd get away with it as well. You know, depression and that? [*laugh*]
> *Wendy:* [*laugh*] what stopped you?

Jane ventures for a second time to express how bad it had felt at times, and I pick up the idea of dying and ask her more. Bion's idea of containment starts with the premise of unconscious intersubjectivity, where emotions are constantly passed between people. He develops the notion that when an idea is too painful to bear because of its associated feeling, the defence of projection is used to get rid of the feeling by putting it into someone else. That person then experiences it through empathy. If it is also too painful for the other person, the person throws it out again quickly, or denies its painfulness, for example by reassurance. If, on the other hand, the other person can contain the pain, it can be returned 'detoxified' and faced as an aspect of reality (see Hollway, 1999). As I contained the painful aspects of Jane's story, she could increasingly face more of it herself. In doing so, as we saw in the above extract, she could remember that it was not that she wanted to die, but that she wanted to be finally rid of him. In my containment of Jane's painful memories, they became safer to acknowledge, which then also enabled her to feel recognised, to feel that her meanings had been emotionally understood.[14]

It was not until quite near the end of the second interview, when I had just explained that I was shifting to the final set of more structured questions, that Jane asked me a question:

Jane: What's it – you know like all this background?
Wendy: Yeah.
Jane: What's it got to do with crime?

This suggests both that she had enough confidence to challenge the ongoing definition of the interview situation and also that she had been wondering, perhaps for some while, why I should want all this information. I answered at length, in terms of the wider things that make people anxious, as in her case. I also said that the crimes that tend to affect women most are things like a violent partner. I finished by saying:

Wendy: You're absolutely right to ask it, you know. [*laughs*] Hope you don't mind.
Jane: No [*laughs*].
Wendy: I mean obviously if there's anything you don't want to say then you just say that you don't want to.
Jane: No it's only mum who knows about – but nobody knows everything.

We will discuss the ethical implications concerning informed consent in this kind of interviewing in Chapter 5. Here, I want to point out that, after this point, Jane became more in control of the interview. She talked about things that were significant to her, notably her mother, and did not bring everything back round to her fear of crime, as she presumably had felt obliged to do by the initial framework in which the interview had been set.

Mother–daughter transference and countertransference

By 'nobody knows everything', Jane seemed to be telling me both that she had not told anyone the full story of her relationship with her violent boyfriend and its aftermath and also that she had told me as much as anyone. The latter suggestion was supported after the tape had been turned off at the end of the interview when she repeated that the only other person she had told this to was her mother. This created a strong parallel between her mother and me in terms of what could be revealed (though not in terms of how upset her mother became).

Another detail contributes to the picture of our mutual unconscious positioning as 'mother' and 'daughter'. Her children were with us – though the young one was often asleep – throughout the interviews, constantly interrupting, checking me out. Rather than ignoring their presence, I talked to the older child from time to time. I explained to be careful of the microphone, told him he was being very patient and that I wouldn't take too much longer, for example. In these ways I positioned myself in a (grand)motherly role in relation to them. I also witnessed her calm and loving relationship to her children and identified with her as a mother.

There was one place later in the text where I was surprised by my change of tone and felt, therefore, that it was worth considering the dynamic at this point. Jane had again claimed that 'it 'asn't really affected me that much' and gone on to wonder if 'I might have blocked it off, I don't know.' She went on to reappraise her denial:[15]

Jane: I suppose it 'as changed me a bit, 'cos I don't like getting involved with anybody ... not properly involved.
Wendy: Mmm.
Jane: Just like being on me own, I think.
Wendy: Mmm. Well a lot of women don't learn that till later on [*Jane*: Na], a lot later on.
Jane: Mum says everything's 'appened all at once.

Normally I would censor as inappropriate this intrusion of my beliefs or experiences into the research relationship. However, encouraged perhaps by wanting to reflect positively on her growing independence, I gave an opinion which positioned me as a woman of a different generation with experience of those kinds of feelings. She then associated my idea to her mother's opinion about what had happened to her, again suggesting that she was making links between us.

From then on in the transcript, she brought back the talk to her mother several times, even though by that time I was going through the structured schedule of questions which we used at the end, and therefore it was more difficult for her to control the subject matter. Her older son was also getting fed up and it was difficult to concentrate for both of us. When I came to the question 'Have you been moved by something recently?' she told me how, recently, her mother had remembered being abused by her (the mother's) father as a child. It seems to me that her telling me this was a product of the relationship we had achieved by this late stage of the interview. She told me this in the context of her mother starting college, finding her 'own independence', attending a women's group, and her tutor telling her it was possible because she was 'getting stronger'. This followed my comment about women finding out eventually that they can be on their own. There were identifications between Jane and me, mutually involving the positions of mother and daughter and encouraging her to think about her mother.

What Jane told me was a co-production. However, she was referring to a prior reality. As Aron (1996) argues in the case of psychoanalysis in the following quotation, so for research interviewing: 'Just because we claim that both patient and analyst play a substantial role in constructing what they agree to be the truth, we need not deny that reality itself has its own structure apart from that which we impose on it' (Aron, 1996: 29). Whether and how Jane's story could be told was dependent upon how we both related to each other up to that point. Irrespective of our differences, I felt moved by the stories of this courageous young woman and admired her caring attitude with her children. These feelings on my side manifested as difficulty in leaving and a strong desire to help. On her side, I can only guess that she regretted that she could not talk more about her mother's experience of sexual abuse and her own feelings about that (she repeated three times how upset she had been by the discovery). I think that it was in an unconscious relation to this that I 'had difficulty disconnecting' (as I wrote in my field notes) and wanted to stay and talk.

With these few examples, we hope it is clear how unconscious inter-subjective dynamics, including mother and daughter transferences and countertransferences, were affecting the research relationship. How does this affect the knowledge which is produced through research interviewing? Ogden (1994) understands the subject as dynamically produced in each intersubjective relationship. He explores the idea of 'finding yourself becoming a subject whom you have not met, but nonetheless recognise' by the process of 'creating a voice with which to speak (think) the words (thoughts) comprising it' (Ogden, 1994: 1). The person who is produced in the interview is, in this sense, new (but also recognisable). It is on such data that we rely as researchers. In the next chapter we turn to the question of analysing data, using the principles of a defended subject, while not losing sight of the social context of interviewees' accounts.

Summary

- The chapter charts developments from our initial pilot attempts using a structured interview schedule through our adaptation of the biographical-interpretative method to our free-association narrative interviewing. The mistakes in our initial pilot interviews resulted from using a highly structured, question-and-answer dominated interview schedule.
- We suggested how four different approaches to interviewing (traditional, feminist, narrative and clinical) might understand this. Only the last of these posited a defended subject.
- We introduced our discovery of the biographical-interpretative method and outlined its four interviewing principles designed to facilitate the production of interviewees' meaning-frames (or *Gestalts*), namely: use open questions, elicit stories, avoid 'why' questions and follow respondents' ordering and phrasing.
- We argued for the importance of free association in adapting the biographical-interpretative method to accommodate our principle of a defended subject.
- Using two extracts from interview transcripts, we demonstrated the ability of our free-association narrative interview to reveal significant personal meanings.
- We illustrated the idea of data as a co-production of the interview pair, in which unconscious intersubjective dynamics were operating: in particular, we illustrated the dynamics of recognition and containment.

Notes

1　For an early example of the former, see Reason and Rowan (1981). Oakley (1982) wrote the classic feminist critique of interviewing. Maynard (1994) provides an overview of feminist methodological critiques. Mishler (1986) also argues for the principle of empowerment of interviewees in social research.

2　As this was a pilot study, both authors were present. Moreover, though Tony hardly knew Ann, she was well known to Wendy. This probably mitigated Tony's 'unknownness', at least to some extent. It also meant that we had wider knowledge of Ann with which to understand the account produced in the interview itself.

3　Thanks to Dave Gadd for this suggestion.

4　Alternatively stories are seen as having a 'setting, problem, plan of action and out-come' (Mishler, 1986: 92). A more complex model of the structure of stories comes from Labov (1972), cited in Mishler (1986: 80–1): abstract, orientation, complicating action, evaluation, result or resolution and coda.

5　This is not always the question. Rosenthal (1993: 71) asked what were, in effect, psychological questions in her research on coming to terms with the interviewees' National Socialist past.

6   Psychoanalysis has many strands. This claim deviates from a classical Freudian emphasis, owing more to Melanie Klein. The emphasis is consistent with our interest in the fear of crime. Of course, by asking about anxiety, we ensured that it emerged as a central facet in people's accounts. However, by asking for stories, not explanation, interviewees were enabled to talk about anxiety in a way that was meaningful in their lives and without just reproducing our own discourse.

7   See Chapter 5 for information about the context of this interview.

8   We found this often to be the case, but it was usually not until we had familiarised ourselves with the whole two interviews that we recognised it. It is an example of the whole giving extra meaning to a part.

9   Our research design included asking whether respondents had relatives on the estate and, where possible, interviewing them. This raised a series of particular ethical problems concerned with confidentiality which we consider in Chapter 5.

10   But, for a further, more detailed look at Tommy and his family of origin, see Chapter 4 and Hollway and Jefferson (1999).

11   We had a prompt sheet so that we said broadly similar things to everyone we asked. We will discuss the issue of informed consent in this kind of interviewing in Chapter 5.

12   Walkerdine talks about her powerful reminders of her working-class childhood when she went into a working-class family for research, but goes on to point out that 'the father in particular saw, not a working-class child but a middle-class adult' (1997: 66).

13   See Benjamin (1995) for a theorisation of recognition and Hinshelwood (1991) for an account of the development of the concept of containment within psychoanalysis.

14   This analysis leads to very different principles for dealing with painful topics than are usually recommended. It is common for interviewers to offer to terminate the interview if the interviewee gets upset. In this light such an approach smacks more of the interviewer escaping from a difficult situation than acting in the interviewee's interests.

15   As with Joyce in Chapter 2, this can be analysed in terms of Jane struggling to achieve a depressive position regarding a painful part of her reality, instead of maintaining a denial. This example shows this being achieved in relation to someone, intersubjectively, rather than as an individual act.

CHAPTER 4

ANALYSING DATA PRODUCED WITH DEFENDED SUBJECTS

The four core questions associated with analysing any qualitative data are:

- what do we notice?
- why do we notice what we notice?
- how can we interpret what we notice?
- how can we know that our interpretation is the 'right' one?

In this chapter, we shall explore the implications of these questions when analysing material produced with defended subjects.[1] Specifically, this entails:

- an extended discussion of a short extract about Tommy's childhood;
- a consideration of the problems of fragmenting qualitative data;
- an illustration of how our holistic approach to Ivy's interview material assisted our interpretations of her relationship to sexual respectability;
- a look at how our theoretical approach is both similar to and different from that used in clinical psychoanalysis, and what sort of knowledge it is capable of producing.

A discussion of Tommy's childhood

Tony: What was it like growing up in such a large family with

Tommy [interrupting]: it were great … You know wi' us being a big family, and everybody, and all at school … We, we always used to race 'ome for cow pie … big meat potato pie – that's when we 'ad coal fires as well … They were the *best* fires that we've ever 'ad, and we all used to race 'ome at tea time, to see who got [*laugh*] biggest plate and everything. We used to 'ave some right arguments, to see who got [*laugh*] biggest plate! And 'Is there, any more, is there, is there any more?' It were brilliant. And sleeping arrangement – 'cos it … were a three-bedroomed 'ouse, between ten of us … Well it were brilliant. [*Tony: laugh*]. There were – one, one, two, there were six of us. Three in one double bed, no, two, two in each double bed. [*Tony:* Yeah.] And in, well, you know then, we were skint. [*Tony:* Yeah] In the 60s we were skint. [*Tony:* Yeah]. And to get a, to get a blanket to get covered up were unbelievable. To get big, big, big overcoats.

[*Tony*: Yeah, yeah.] What me mother used to do, you, you know plates in oven – she used to put some bricks in. Get bricks out – t' warm bottom, warm bottom of the bed. And get plate out of oven, wrap it up in a er, a, a, a sheet and put it in bottom of bed, so stretch your feet out. And it were, it were, it were 'orrible in the morning 'cos it were, it were freezing cold. [*Tony*: Yeah.] Y'know plate and brick. There were no double glazing, no central 'eating or anything. All we, all we lived for were coal fire. [*Tony*: Yeah.] And me dad used to get up every morning, make s- sticks out of paper. [*Tony*: Yeah.] About 6 o'clock. Used to get *fire* blaring out before we get up … Always used to run down for a cup of tea, run at side of fire … They were tremendous years.

The above question and answer took place during the second interview between Tommy (who you met in Chapter 3) and Tony Jefferson. Our exploration of the four core questions will proceed through a series of stages. It will start with a critical look at the 'tell it like it is' common-sense approach, continue with an illustration of the importance of using evidence from the whole context,[2] and end by showing how adequate meanings can only be produced from data by utilising theory and by using reflexivity. But, before we take you through our analysis, write down what you noticed in the above account, and why; then compare both with what follows.

The 'tell it like it is' common-sense approach

If we take this account at face value it is a variation of the 'we were poor but we were happy' story of life in a big, crowded household. In other words, what we notice in a common-sense fashion is the overt content of the account: how Tommy appears to have thoroughly enjoyed his childhood, despite plenty of evidence of deprivation ('is there any more?'; 'it were 'orrible in the morning 'cos it were … freezing cold'), hardship (two in a bed, overcoats for blankets) and poverty ('we were skint'). Indeed, if we take him at his words, which echo like a chorus throughout his account, his childhood was 'great … brilliant … unbelievable … tremendous'. Thus, for those 'tell it like it is' ethnographers and others, for whom the analytic task consists of little more than giving a voice to their informants, Tommy's story is one of a happy childhood. What Tommy tells is what Tommy is; the analytic task is to assist in the production of Tommy's voice, not to assume the stance of interpreter which implies knowing better than Tommy.

The problem with this level of noticing is that it is insufficiently attentive both to detail and to contradictions. In the above account, for example, the detail of how and when Tommy first utters 'it were great' is revealing since it bursts forth from Tommy's mouth, interrupting the interviewer's opening question. Why so hasty, we should ask? One reason for inordinate haste is to pre-empt alternative suggestions: in this case Tommy might be pre-empting any hint of pity that the interviewer might be harbouring, or of a less positive image of the difficulties of life in large, poor families. This apparent need to ensure a particular reading of his childhood may well have been exacerbated by his perception of class difference, since he was a long-term unemployed man living on the 'difficult to let' end of a high-crime, council estate and the interviewer, apparently, an educated, middle-class researcher from the local university. (See the section on 'Using reflexivity' below for an extended exploration of the relationship between Tommy and the interviewer.) Having noted this, the subsequent chorus of how 'brilliant' it all was begins to feel a little forced; a case perhaps of protesting too much? Read in this way – in a way which gives more weight to the ''orrible' dimension of these memories – we might be less convinced about how 'great' it all was, and more inclined to hold on to a theme about kids fighting for survival in a deprived, poverty-stricken household: racing home from school in order to get enough to eat, constantly wanting more, fighting over blankets (or overcoats) to keep warm at night, and waking up 'freezing cold' and running down to secure a (no doubt also contested) place by the fire.

One reason for these failures of noticing is the commitment to allowing informants their voice, to tell (us) how it is (for them). Since most of us offer accounts of our lives which accentuate consistency and suppress contradiction, in the interests of producing a coherent, rational self, the 'tell it like it is' interviewer, in effect, reproduces such a self. In other words, data analysis is driven by the rationalising self-descriptions of informants, which are also the touchstone for judging the correctness of any interpretation. Within this self-justifying circle, in which the interviewee serves as both data and interpretative check, the failure to notice inconsistencies, contradictions, changes of tone and other textual interruptions is necessarily endemic. As we shall see in the next section, this approach would overlook or ignore a lot of evidence scattered around in the data.

Evidence: the whole context

There are various ways in which we want to argue for the importance of the whole in understanding a part. For the moment, though, we wish to focus on the most straightforward meaning, namely, that of using the whole of the data we produced relating to Tommy to assist the interpretation of the part discussed above, the extract about his childhood. To do this involved thoroughly familiarising ourselves with the rest of the interview transcript material (nearly 300 pages if we include those derived from interviews with his sister Kelly and mother

Ivy) to see what other pieces of evidence there were which might help resolve the issue of whether Tommy's childhood was brilliant, or awful, or something else again.

This familiarisation with all the relevant transcripts produced lots more evidence supporting the idea that Tommy's childhood was difficult and harsh, and little evidence to the contrary. In addition to food, warmth, space and money being in short supply, Tommy could not remember being kissed as a child, an indication that parental affection of a physical kind may well have been in short supply too (and continues, apparently, since Tommy claimed he never kisses his mother even now, despite being close to her and seeing her frequently). However, physical punishment was not in short supply (*Ivy*: 'they've 'ad some 'ammer off me – them I've got'), which included getting 'whacked' with his dad's belt. It is a family where, according to Ivy, she was out frequently ('I never stopped in once before I were ill … I used to go out seven nights a week to bingo')[3] and was both a fighter ('oh I used to fight. They take after me') and a drinker ('I used to be a big drinker … I used to be drunk every night'). Dad was working nights, sleeping days or also out drinking after the day shift ('' e went out for a drink you see when 'e came 'ome at night, which as you couldn't blame 'im'). Later, the shame of two of Tommy's older sisters' teenage pregnancies appeared to precipitate their mother's breakdown and subsequent agoraphobia (see below), and at least four of the children got into trouble with the law, two seriously enough to warrant terms of imprisonment. One of them, his sister Fiona, seems to have been chronically delinquent. Ivy claimed to have had her 'put down three or four times'.

We do not wish to suggest that Tommy did not have good times, even 'brilliant' times as a child. Nor are we suggesting that he is incapable of recognising the ' 'orrible' dimension to his childhood. But what this broader look at the whole of the evidence revealed, consistently, is Tommy's inability to acknowledge the emotional reality – the pain – of these memories, unlike his sister Kelly who 'hated' her childhood and could not get away soon enough. If, then, the evidence suggests that Tommy's judgement on his childhood should not be taken at face value, and that his characteristically upbeat memories around his childhood and family are one-sided, how can we interpret this evidence in a more satisfactory way?

Utilising theory

We have already seen how the 'tell it like it is' approach to social-science research is committed to representing interviewees' voices, a commitment which, as we argued above, eliminates any meaningful distinction between description and theoretical interpretation. We have also argued that this commitment would tend, in Tommy's case, to echo Tommy's own one-sidedness. So, why is it that we noticed what our interviewee did not? The answer is to be found in our theory of the defended subject in which the crucial motivation for investment in particular discourses is the need to defend oneself against feelings of anxiety. All interpretative work, however sociological, requires a theory of the subject, though it may be implicit rather than explicit. Let's see how our principle of the defended subject makes better sense of Tommy, remembering that our notion is not narrowly psychoanalytic but psychosocial.[4]

Recall how, in Chapter 2, we discussed Roger's investment in a discourse of an idealised past – the 'golden age' – despite evidence suggesting that his past had been less than ideal, notably his experience of his father's brutality. We explained this in terms of the defensive function such an investment performed. In legitimating and therefore mitigating his painful childhood experiences, it defended him from them. We went on to talk of his idealisation of the past and denigration of the present as an example of the paranoid-schizoid splitting of good and bad, and how such splitting protected him, an ageing, ailing man, from having to face up to his loss of any meaningful patriarchal authority in his present life.

By positing a similar defensive pattern we can begin to make sense of Tommy's idealisation of his childhood. As with Roger, Tommy denies the harsher realities of his past. He splits the bad from the good in order to protect his present self. Why he needs to do this we shall come to shortly. The above extract from Tommy demonstrates his mind simultaneously adopting two inconsistent points of view (one in the detail and an opposite one in his generalised claim). Does he also, like Roger, split good and bad and locate them in external objects? If the good and the bad have been separated, and the good has become located in an idealised version of childhood, where has the bad ended up?

Unlike Roger, Tommy did not denigrate the estate; in fact, he loved it, despite acknowledging that 'it's terrible'. Nor did he demonise particular groups on it, since for him the problem was 'kids', and parents failing to control them. Perhaps surprisingly, given the role of family in his defensive idealisation, it was a family member, his younger sister Kelly (whom we meet in Chapter 6), who seemed to be the recipient of his negative projections: 'the only one in the family I 'ate' (a point he makes three times). 'I love everybody else.' It is through such splitting that his investment in his fantastic family can be sustained, which he explains through the common-sense discourse about all families having one 'black sheep': 'There's always one in a family … Like I've told you, there's my sister in my family.'

Our interpretation that Tommy's hatred of his sister is an example of his tendency to split the good from the bad for defensive purposes had, like all our interpretations, to be justified. Had she done terrible things which could explain Tommy's hatred? Only when we had exhausted such possibilities did we begin to regard this as an example of Tommy's defensive splitting. When we allowed that possibility we found it enabled us to illuminate other aspects of Tommy's behaviour: like throwing a stone in a pond, if an interpretation 'works' the ripples reverberate through the rest of the analysis. When interpretations do this, when they illuminate other data beyond their starting-point, our faith in their robustness can increase correspondingly. By exploring Tommy as a defended subject, evidenced especially through the denigration of his sister Kelly, we hope to show something of this process: of the movement from inadequate to more useful explanations, and the exponential benefits of good interpretations.

The stated reason for Tommy's hatred of Kelly is that 'she's grown up to be a big 'ead and such a liar'. Only two specific examples of these claimed faults are given (though it is worth noting that Kelly herself admitted lying to the family about the violence she was subjected to – a demonstration, should one be needed, that lying is not necessarily a hateworthy offence). In the first example, Tommy claimed 'she's forged my mother's signature to draw some money out of this bank book which makes her an evil woman ... to do it to 'er own mother.' Whether true or not, we already knew that Kelly's relations with her mother Ivy were difficult and complex. We can suppose, therefore, that, if true, there is more to this story than Tommy knows, or is prepared to know. We also supposed that Tommy's source for this story was his mother, with her own investments in imagining, and retelling, the worst about Kelly. So, we should notice Tommy's preparedness to side with his mother, to recount only her version and hence believe the worst about his sister. His other specific charge is that Kelly 'takes 'er three kids round [to Ivy's], "look after kids while I go to work" but she never gives 'er a penny'. He, on the other hand, buys her 'stuff every weekend'. We were familiar with the first part of this complaint, having learned of it earlier through Ivy. We know that the reasons for Kelly 'exploiting' her mother in this way have deep roots (which concerned all the child care Kelly was forced to do[5] which, she felt, robbed her of her childhood and teenage years), and notice Tommy echoing his mother's complaint, seeing it only through her eyes. The other side of his sister's 'exploitation' of his mother is, in Tommy's eyes, his own generosity in this respect: where Kelly takes, he gives. Here, perhaps, a certain sibling rivalry or jealousy over Ivy's response to Kelly's child-care needs is fuelling Tommy's hatred (even though Tommy's son gets to stop over too).

Even if these one-sided accounts are true, and Kelly is now a big-headed liar, hatred seems disproportionate. Kelly is the little sister

Tommy 'learnt … to walk when she were a baby'; who endured a horrendously violent relationship which almost killed her, and after which he and his brothers supported her. It also seems irrational when we consider his apparent ability to forgive all kinds of faults in other family members. His sister Fiona, for example, with her troubled history of early pregnancy, delinquency and spells of imprisonment, would appear to have done far more to damage the family name than Kelly. An outsider would make Fiona, not Kelly, the problem member of the family, if one is going to use such terms. But Tommy, even knowing 'she just was a waste of time', still loves Fiona. In her case, others get the blame: 'she just went wi' wrong people.'[6]

Given this evidence of Tommy denying the negative, painful aspects of Fiona's behaviour, but not granting the same tolerance to little sister Kelly, we concluded that such irrationality demonstrated splitting behaviour. However, it was only when we were able to answer the question of how Tommy's denigration of Kelly functioned to protect his self-identity, why she and not Fiona became the receptacle for his bad feelings, that we thought we were on to something important about Tommy – because with that knowledge a whole lot of other things we knew about him began to make fuller sense. In other words, we needed to be able to answer the question of why Tommy was invested in the denigration of Kelly to be sure that we were witnessing an example of defensive splitting. Answering this riddle, we found, was only possible when we presupposed not only a defended subject but a psychosocial one as well. It hinges on Tommy's relation to respect.

A history of the English working classes could be written focused through the importance of a series of bipolar divisions: labouring versus dangerous classes; deserving versus undeserving poor; industrial proletariat versus lumpenproletariat; skilled versus unskilled; employed versus unemployed; respectable versus rough. Some of these distinctions have had their heyday (who now talks of the dangerous classes?), though many, like the distinction between the deserving and undeserving poor, continue to haunt public debate (Murray, 1990). At one time, the notion of the respectable working-class man[7] connoted permanent (not casual), skilled employment, heterosexuality, marriage, clean-living, sobriety, moderation and reliable provision for, and protection of, the family (religion optional). More recently, and particularly as a consequence of de-industrialisation, some of these linkages, such as that between permanent skilled employment and respectability, have become seriously, if not fatally, attenuated. Tommy, as we shall see, belongs to the next generation: the one that has never properly worked. Yet, the theme of respect remains important to him.

Before looking at the evidence for this, we need to mention briefly the relation between respect and respectability. There is, of course, a connection as implied by the shared root, but there is also an important difference. As with the different way respectability connotes for men and women, with sexual status crucial for women's respectability, the difference between respect and respectability also implicates gender. For men, respect, in its meaning 'to treat ... with deference, esteem or honour' (*Shorter Oxford English Dictionary*), is arguably the most endur-ing cross-cultural feature of contemporary masculinity; it applies regard-less of respectability. Thus, the delinquent gang member who has been 'dissed' (disrespected) on the street and the mafia boss who has been insulted by a rival share with the working man a concern to 'be respected'; this is something they share by virtue of being men having to relate to the issue of masculine 'honour'. Respectability has other origins. Its contemporary meaning of 'those features of life and con-duct which are regarded as respectable' (*Shorter OED*) were forged from a nineteenth-century meeting of minds between labouring men keen to be accepted in bourgeois society and a ruling alliance wanting to encourage incorporation. This is too crude to capture the vicissitudes of linguistic terms in use in a constantly changing world, but it is a warning against a simple elision of respect/respectability, which we try to avoid in what follows.[8]

Tommy's concern with 'being respected' emerges early in our first interview, and recurs throughout his talk about both his father's and his own standing in the community. Wondering why he has not been a victim of crime in his 33 years on the 'rougher' end of the estate, he suggests it is 'Because we're well respected. We've been well respected on this estate ever since we've moved up.' Later, when Tommy was asked how it felt moving on to the estate (when he was nine years old), he talked of feeling 'right proud':

> *Tommy:* It were brilliant feeling, to move into – and to move into a big 'ouse,
> 'cos it 'ad got a parlour, parlour-type room. [*Tony:* Yeah.] It were fantastic.
> And I felt right, right cocky ... the estate were unbelievable. People com-
> ing out, 'do you want any 'elp? ... Do you want a drink of tea?' ... Leave
> your door open na, they're in straight away, take your television and
> video. To walk up on this estate, I felt right proud. Because it – it was a
> ten-year waiting list for a three-bedroom and a five-year waiting list for a
> two-bedroom. Na they can't wait to get off estate and nobody wants to
> come and live on estate.[9]

This 'cocky' pride in moving into a 'big 'ouse' with a 'parlour-type room', for which there was a five- or ten-year waiting list, says that for the young Tommy this was a step up in the world. We also know that his move was part of an inner-city slum clearance operation, which adds weight to the interpretation. Put in terms of respectability, for a large, poor family moving from inner-city slums, moving on to a much sought-after estate (as it was at that time), this was likely to be seen in terms of a movement towards respectability from the label 'rough' to which such families are prone. Tommy's pride, then, was probably an internalisation of a family pride in having moved closer to respectability by virtue of their move; set within this context, the meaning of the family being 'well respected' would seem to imply being respected *for their respectability*.

In the second interview, Tommy uses identical terms to talk of his dead father:

> *Tommy:*   He were, he were well respected chap. [*Tony*: Mmm.] They still talk about 'im in in club where we go into na. 'There were nobody, there were nobody better than your dad, your dad were fantastic.'

Whether 'well respected' here connotes masculine honour (Tommy is referring to a working men's club) or family respectability (in the sense of 'features of life and conduct'), or both, is unclear. However, the fact that Albert was a steadfast, hard-working family man who was strict with his children probably qualified him for the term 'respectable' on the estate.

If one basis for his father being well respected was the fact that he worked 13-hour shifts in the local steelworks to support a large family, and died too young to enjoy the fruits of his long labours ('never got … not even got 'is bus pass'), this basis for respect was denied to Tommy. He left school in the late 1960s, served a seven-year apprenticeship, after which the firm 'went bust'. Thereafter, a series of short-term jobs followed, each ending in redundancy, interspersed with a two-year period of unemployment. His last job ended after 18 months when the forge closed. He was in his late twenties. He has never worked since.

So, external changes in the world of work, with Tommy one of the early casualties of de-industrialisation, left him having to seek alternative bases upon which to build respect. One basis is community involvement. Since he met his current partner he has become involved in the local working men's club, where he is a life member and current President: '[I] built meself up' and got a 'reputation'. Now he is well respected there. Another potential arena for securing respect is family life. A sense of the strength of this investment is captured movingly in his emotional response to being asked whether he would be 'grandad' to his eldest stepson's first child: 'And I went "I'd love it." I just broke down. 'im asking me.'

A third basis for Tommy's sense of self-respect is embedded, if somewhat opaquely, in the following extract:

> *Tommy:*   I don't think anything will 'appen to me while I'm on this estate. [*Tony*: Right.] 'cos I've, I've confidence I've, I've got, I've got respect. I respect everybody on this estate. There's, there's kiddies all o'er this estate all call me by me first name … It's brilliant. [*Tony*: Mmm.] Wherever you go 'hi ya Tommy, alright Tommy?' I love it. But I don't fear. I don't fear, fear anything. Nobody 'll touch me. [*Tony*: Right.] I'm well respected. And

> I respect, I respect all families on estate. I know, I know what they are, but
> you can't do anything about it. All you do is, you go and see their parents.

What does it mean to talk not only of being respected but of respecting 'everybody'? Given that he knows 'what they are', a reference to the rampant delinquency of many of the youngsters on the estate, this apparently universal respect may seem merely another example of his characteristic defence of idealisation; as does the notion that kids calling him by his first name is 'brilliant'.[10] But in a world where the prospects of socially valued achievements are few, where de-industrialisation and other changes are denying this generation of men their expected patrimonial inheritance, knowing others and being known becomes part of what being well respected means. Saying 'good morning to anybody ... no matter who it is' and always getting a good morning back is a sign of being well respected, as is talking to someone who knew his father. 'I've got respect. I respect everybody on this estate' is about knowing and being known: Tommy has respect in the sense that everybody knows him; he respects everybody, meaning he knows everybody. In this discursive frame, respect signifies the direct opposite of getting on and moving out, as in Kelly's version of respectability (see Chapter 6).

Now we can return to the question of why Tommy is so invested in the denigration of Kelly. This links with why he identifies with his mother in the way that they both view Kelly as a 'liar and a big 'ead'. It also bears on why it is that he and his sister have come to hold such diametrically opposed notions of respect/ability with Tommy's cen-tred in his family of origin and the estate he loves and Kelly's on dis-tancing her new family from both her family of origin and the estate. Tommy was proud when he moved on to the estate, and 33 years later he still loves it, 'even though it's terrible' and nobody wants to live there anymore. The estate, for all its problems, is practically the only place he's ever known; it's where he is known and belongs, like his father before him; it's where he feels safe; it's where he's destined to remain ('unless I win pools'); and, as a long-term unemployed man with few prospects of meaningful work, it has to be his best prospect of achieving 'respect'.

Being unable to move, either geographically or socially, reinforces Tommy's habitual pattern of denying the negative features of his family and the estate. His sense of self-worth and respect necessarily implicates the very family and community that Kelly has rejected. Because Tommy's self-respect depends on what Kelly has rejected, he cannot afford, either psychically or socially, to recognise why Kelly must embrace her particular version of respectability. Since the costs are too high, he pathologises her choice, hating her for rejecting him, them, the estate. Her big headedness is just that: too big for these things he is invested in. Kelly is not only rejected, but hated for aiming for what he does not, and cannot, have.

Using reflexivity

Utilising our particular theory of the subject has enabled us to answer two conundrums posed by Tommy – his idealisation of his past and hostility to sister Kelly – and to connect these to his investment in an estate-based version of respect. However, this would have been less easy had I (Tony, since I was the interviewer) not also deployed my own subjectivity to assist the analysis. Using reflexivity in this way can serve both to guard against bad interpretations and to assist with good ones. What distinguishes between good and bad use of reflexivity is obviously a vexed question for social science. Clinical psychoanalysis has been facing this question for longer, having acknowledged the impossibility of scientific objectivity earlier.[11] We discuss the ramifications of this question at many points in this book. What I wish to demonstrate in this section is how certain biographical similarities between me and Tommy assisted my noticing and hence our analysis.

My notes on initial impressions say that Tommy was 'slightly guarded' when first approached and had a 'clean, well-kept' appearance – and a car to match: 'old, but immaculately kept'. After the first interview, I noted that 'rapport seemed good', and that he 'was quite physical with me [a reference to his willingness to touch me during the interview from time to time], suggesting some ease'. After the second interview, I noted that 'rapport felt very good (he called me Tony)' and that he was 'clearly interested in [the] project'. A big reason for this good rapport, I felt, stemmed from our both being members of big families. He never knew that about me, but listening to him talking about his family produced points of identification which to some extent bridged our class, educational and work differences, probably enabling me to be a better, more informed listener. His clean, tidy, well-kept house (unlike some we entered), his active involvement in community affairs, including running a local kids' football team and refereeing local matches, and his apparent fitness (in stark contrast to the poor physical shape of many men of his age we interviewed on the estate), also facilitated my identification with him (my past includes a spell as a PE teacher). In short, I enjoyed interviewing Tommy because I liked him; and I liked him because we had things in common.

Of course, the differences of class, education and conventional signs of success must have been stark to Tommy, though I always arrived on foot and in casual dress (it was summer) partly to minimise these. On appearances alone, an outsider would have been hard-pressed to pick out the researcher in the room. On reading the transcripts, I noticed more differences – he was more conservative and cautious than my initial impressions, for example – which led me to feel less warm in retrospect than I had felt when in direct contact with him. But the issue here is how I was able to deploy my subjective knowledge of life in a big, hard-up family to assist our interpretation of Tommy's account.

Let us return to our opening extract. Our theoretical starting-point was undoubtedly important in alerting us to the contradictory nature of Tommy's account, but so too was my subjective feeling on reading it; how disjunctive it felt to my experience. Since I come from a family of seven children, living in a three-bedroomed house with parents struggling to make ends meet, Tommy's scenario was all too familiar: cold bedrooms (freezing in winter), shared beds, mealtime arguments, stretching scarce food around ever-hungry mouths (my mother's attempts to make food last longer included hiding the always scarce biscuits). It certainly had its 'laughs', its funny side (the family refrain was 'if you don't laugh about it you'd cry'), but nobody will convince me that life in a large, hard-up family is great *because* of the accompanying deprivations, as Tommy seemed to insist, rather than *despite* them, which is of course a possibility.

It might be objected that my memories are no more reliable than Tommy's and that I am projecting on to him my own feelings about unpleasant aspects of my childhood. This possibility can be tested against Tommy's text: am I providing the negative aspects or are they present? Our judgement is that they are present in the detail but shorn of the emotion which would naturally accompany them. It is that accompaniment that I feel I know and can use empathically here. We also made use of our different subjectivities as a way of triangulating on the data we interpreted: did Wendy, from a very different family background, agree that this interpretation applied to Tommy, rather than belonging in part to me?

Let me use a second example concerning Tommy's strict father, Albert, since my father, too, was strict. Though his mother claimed she 'did the 'itting', and that Albert didn't (' 'e would correct 'em, but if they wanted 'itting, it were me'), Tommy remembered otherwise:

> *Tommy:*   Got a leather belt like that and a big brass buckle on end, and 'e'd say 'If you're not in for 8 o'clock, you gets the strap. If you don't do as you're told, you'll get the buckle.' And we 'ad to be in 'ouse for 8 o'clock. I was in bed for half past eight. [*Tony:* Mmm.] And any murmur up them stairs – 'e used to run upstairs me dad. I thought, 'ere we go, get 'old, get 'old of blankets and get covered up, 'cos we're gonna get whacked with his belt. And 'e used to come up and whack us with his belt. [*Tony:* He did?] Oh, unbelievable, aye. But appreciated 'im for it because 'e knocked, 'e knocked, 'e knocked sense into us, not to do it. But er, I, we were growing up, growing up, we 'ad some laughs.

This is a common tale of paternal beatings: we heard many similar in the course of our interviews. My father never used a belt, but otherwise Albert could have been my dad racing up the stairs when the noise (of the three of us boys in our shared bedroom) got too much for him. When he did so, which, thankfully was not often, it was truly frightening. Tommy's dad used a belt, surely a more terrifying prospect than that of a 'spanking'. But the fear, and the pain of being 'whacked with his belt', has been erased from the account. There is no hint that such punishment ever felt cruel, unjust or excessive (despite the evidence that such beltings could be the result (as were ours) merely of talking in bed: 'any murmer up them stairs'); only feelings of gratitude ('appreciated 'im for it') and memories of good times ('we 'ad some laughs'). For me and my brothers, our punishments often felt unjust and excessive ('we were only talking' or 'only playing with a ball' would be our constant 'excuse'). Later I could afford to be more understanding. I could begin to comprehend how a father, tired after a long day's work, with money and other worries on his mind, wanting only a bit of peace and quiet and some quality time with his wife, could overreact to the boisterousness of his large family settling down for the night or take it out on them for reasons beyond the misdemeanour in question. But that understanding could never eliminate the terror of father running up the stairs, nor lead me to 'appreciate' him for it.

That knowledge, etched into my subjective experience, meant I read Tommy's extract in disbelief. Later the theory helped us to make better sense of it. Because I felt terrified, does it necessarily mean that Tommy did? There are two criteria against which to judge. First, there is the theoretical question of whether intentional physical violence is always a violation and therefore of emotional significance, even if, as in psychoanalytic theory, that emotional significance is hidden. Then there is the empirical question of the evidence within Tommy's account: he hid under the bedclothes to protect himself from the pain of the belt.

Using reflexivity is not a substitute for utilising theory. But, as the above examples show, it can strengthen a theoretical conviction or alert us to a misreading. Like everything else, subjectivity too must be checked; in the above examples, the more I check back with my experiences, or remember how Roger, who was also the recipient of harsh punishment, referred to his father as a 'cruel old sod', the more I remain convinced that our account of Tommy's splitting makes sense.

This extended discussion of how to analyse Tommy as a psychosocial subject began with an extract about Tommy's childhood. However, in order to make the points we did, we also drew on what we had learned of Tommy from the rest of his interview and other data. In other words, to produce our analysis, we moved between parts and the whole of Tommy's data. Keeping both parts and whole in mind is not easy, partly because of the pressures to break down and code material rather than to try to hang on to its wholeness. In the next section, we consider these difficulties in more detail, and then, in the final section, show the procedures we adopted to keep our subjects wholly in mind and how these assisted our interpretations of Ivy's interview material.

The problems of fragmenting qualitative data

We have already discussed the tendency to remain descriptive in qualitative data analysis (QDA). Here we want to identify the methodological – as opposed to theoretical – reasons for this. We contrast the fragmenting of data with the *Gestalt* principle and use an example to show how we achieved a holistic interpretation of the interviews we conducted with Ivy Walters (Tommy's mother).

Faced with a mass of unstructured data, the urge of any researcher is understandably to break these down using some kind of system. The most common system is the code and retrieve method. As Coffey and Atkinson (1996: 22) comment: 'strategies that are dependent on coding the data and using the codes to retrieve analytically significant segments of data … [are] a common starting point for researchers … The fragmentation of data implied in the coding strategy often leads researchers to overlook the form of their data.' We want to explore further the idea of form in qualitative data and the tradition for this idea is that of *Gestalt*, which, in German, means 'form'.

First, however, it is worth noting that this problem of fragmentation of data is perhaps the most significant weakness in computer-assisted qualitative data analysis (CAQDA). As the developers of the popular NUD*IST packages acknowledge, 'because the code and retrieve method was easily supported by computers [it] became the basis of most specialist QDA software' (Richards and Richards, 1994: 447). One of the results of these packages is 'the common tendency for clerical coding to dominate and analysis to be postponed' (1994: 454). In their assessment of the future of CAQDA they conclude that 'the problem and the excitement is that QDA is probably the most subtle and intuitive of human epistemological enterprises, and therefore likely to be the last to achieve satisfactory computerisation' (1994: 461). It is hard to pin down subtlety and intuition, but we believe that using these capacities is unavoidable once the researcher has posited a psychosocial subject.

The principle of *Gestalt* is based on the idea that the whole is greater than the sum of the parts. Wertheimer, the founder of *Gestalt* psychology, objected to the way that, in his view, modern science proceeded from below to above. He believed that it was impossible to 'achieve an understanding of structured totals by starting with the ingredient parts which enter into them. On the contrary we shall need to understand the structure; we shall need to have insight into it. There is then some possibility that the components themselves will be understood' (cited in Murphy and Kovach, 1972: 258–9). This is the principle which we try to apply to our understanding of the 'whole' text. Wertheimer's primary law, that of 'place in context' (that significance is a function of position in a wider framework), addresses exactly the problem of decontextualisation of text which is inherent in the code and retrieve method. Wertheimer emphasised that 'parts are defined by their relation to the system as a whole in which they are functioning' (Murphy and Kovach, 1972: 258). Similarly, the structuralist movement, which started in social anthropology and linguistics, emphasised that meanings could only be understood in relation to a larger whole, whether it be the culture, the sentence or the narrative.

We recognise that people cannot be totally known, much less that such can be elicited in two interviews. At its simplest, as we show above, our 'whole' is all we have accumulated relating to a particular person who took part in the research. As well as the transcripts from both interviews, we have our memories of our meetings with that person, the notes we took after the first meeting and subsequent interviews and also, where more than one family member was interviewed, what was said about our participant by others. For Ivy, we have all of these sources of data. But this definition refers to an external reality. Perhaps we can appreciate better the *Gestalt* principle if it is understood also as the internal capacity for holding those data together in the mind. CAQDA offers increasingly sophisticated ways of not holding the data as a whole in the mind, precisely because it affords ways of holding it outside the mind. Although it provides a powerful capacity to make links,[12] these links are stored outside the mind and retrieved, from the computer, in smaller parts.

This capacity to hold the whole in the mind has its parallels in the writings of clinical psychoanalysis, and recent connectionist neuropsychology is stressing a similarly *Gestalt*-type principle as the basis of thinking (Wilson, 1997). After a whole day working on the transcripts of a particular participant (a process we often referred to as 'immersion')[13] we would feel inhabited by that person in the sense that our imagination was full of him or her. The impact such work had is best demonstrated by the fact that our interviewees could appear in our dreams and waking fantasies. The process of dreaming about them suggests that our developing insights into a person were not occurring just at a conscious intentional level, but that unconscious processes – our fantasy life and emotions – were also working on that '*Gestalt*'.[14] Psychoanalytic ideas of transference and countertransference (see Chapter 3) and of projective identification[15] refer to this unconscious 'embrace' of another person. Alvarez defines neutrality in the clinical setting in a way that captures our attempts: 'the achievement of sufficient distance from the impact of the patient to think, yet not so much distance that empathic sensitivity and counter-transference receptivity get lost' (1985: 88).

The importance of keeping the whole in mind

While the above stresses the importance of creativity and intuition (important features of subjectivity), it is not advisable to sit and wait for a bolt of inspiration! We used two structured ways of summarising a whole case for further reference: completing a two-page pro forma and writing a pen portrait. We will illustrate the way in which this helped us to grasp the form of Ivy's account below.

The pro forma consisted of categories ranging from standard bio-data to comments on themes and ideas that emerged from the whole reading (see Appendix). During the reading of all the raw data we had, we took notes and possibly highlighted significant extracts from it. From these we filled in the pro forma. The difference between the notes (which we also kept in each person's file) and the pro forma is that the notes were a way of amassing descriptive detail, while the summary was used to begin to convey some kind of whole.

The pen portrait aimed to write something which made the person come alive for a reader. It would be largely descriptive and provide enough information against which subsequent interpretations could be assessed. In a way, a pen portrait serves as a substitute 'whole' for a reader who will not have access to the raw data but who needs to have a grasp of the person who figures in a case study if anything said about him or her is going to be meaningful.

In our view, consistent with a theorisation of the defended subject, it is important for summaries not to iron out inconsistencies, contradictions and puzzles. To grasp a person through the 'whole' of what we know about him or her does not have to imply that he or she is consistent, coherent or rational.[16] The form of a person's accounts (or whatever other data we have about his or her life) may become visible by concentrating on these 'fractures'. We illustrate this with Ivy.

You will already have formed some impression of Ivy since she figures as Tommy's mother, above. Before you go on to read about her, consider what impressions you have already formed about her and how you arrived at them. In any encounter (physical, visual or verbal) with another person, the significance of what you know, and what you feel about what you already know, strives for a form or whole which goes beyond the elements.

We are extracting two themes from our pen portrait of Ivy here (excluding, for these purposes, a lot of material on criminal victimisation, risk and the fear of crime), which at this point were unconnected.

The first is her nervous breakdown and subsequent agoraphobia; the second comprises her relationships with her sons and daughters.

Mother of nine and grandmother of 32, Ivy Walters, aged 70, lives in new, purpose-built accommodation on the same council housing estate where she has spent most of her adult life. She rarely leaves home, not only because of her bad legs (she is considerably over-weight), but because she is agoraphobic and liable to panic attacks when she does go out. Unrelated to anything she could identify, she had a 'nervous breakdown'.

> Ivy: It just got – I were frightened to go out then. Before me 'usband died. I wouldn't go out and peg a pair of socks on line ... 'E [the psychiatrist] asked me what I were frightened on. I said 'I just don't want to go out.' I said 'I don't want to go to shops. I don't want to go on a bus. I don't want to go to Bingo or 'ang anything on line.' He said 'Tell me why.' I said 'I don't know. I just don't want to go.'

Ivy's relationships with her sons and daughters are distinctly different – those with her sons appear to be straightforward but with her daughters full of strong feelings: adoration for the eldest, guilt following early rejection for the middle one and dislike and accusations for the youngest. Ivy's own mother, very old and frail, refuses to see her and one of two other sisters. These themes were already evident in the case summary contained on Ivy's pro forma, surrounded by many other details. For example, information about Ivy's breakdown, agoraphobia and panic attacks was contained under two headings in the case summary: health and anxiety / worry / traumatic events. Under the section on children / grandchildren there was a rich mixture of facts, summary and interpretation:

> Nine children, eight in quick succession, including two sets of boy twins. Thirty-two grandchildren. Very different relationships with the six boys (never criticised, like the father) and the three girls. Idolises eldest, rejected middle one, demonises youngest.

The generalisation about her relationships was supported by many instances in the transcripts, too numerous to mention. For example, the boys were referred to generally: 'I 'ave got good lads.' 'I've not 'ad any trouble with those lads of mine' (not true), but the girls never were. Sally, the eldest, was 'me best lass'; Fiona, the middle one, was returned to again and again in the context of how Ivy couldn't take to her as a child, but now talks every day on the phone, routinely saying 'I love you' in response to Fiona's crying and protestations of love. Ivy refers to Kelly, the youngest, as ' 'er round corner', never by her name. If we had been using computer software, such examples would all have been placed in a file coded something like 'relationships with her children'. The summaries were not just descriptive summaries, however. Our noticing these differences was enhanced by our theoretical familiarity with, in particular, a psychoanalytic literature of the development of gender differences in parent–child relations.

Making a link

This was how far our summaries had got us in understanding Ivy. In *Gestalt* terms, you could say that there were lots of unconnected elements that came – bottom-up fashion – from the data, but that there were many missing links, links which could provide the 'form' to Ivy's account. The puzzle of her unaccounted nervous breakdown made us notice something in a part of the text that was ostensibly an answer to our question about whether Albert, her husband, was a worrier too. A key link could be made in consequence:

> Ivy: And I used to say 'Oh, I'm not going out, people will be talking about me, 'er [daughter Fiona] being pregnant.' He [Albert] used to say 'Let 'em talk about you, while they're talking about you, they're leaving somebody else alone.'
>
> Wendy: [*laugh*] Is that one of the reasons you didn't like to go out?
>
> Ivy: I weren't frightened 'cos I used to show off if anybody said owt. I mean when Fiona were took in 'ospital, er, I 'ad a right go at one of doctors there … And when she were in 'ospital, when she'd 'ad our Jonathan – I went – she wouldn't – I couldn't keep away. I 'ad to be there all the time. And I went in one day and she were crying. I said 'What you crying for?' She said er, 'Two of women have just said – aye that's 'er what's not married.'

Ivy makes a link between people talking about Ivy and Fiona's pregnancy. The link is her fear of this, although she does not say so directly. In other words, Ivy provides both the link and its emotional explanation. She does this unwittingly by free association. Her own relationship to this knowledge is difficult though. When the interviewer picks up on the suggested connection by asking 'Is that one of the reasons you didn't like to go out?', Ivy contradicts the previous unwitting suggestion with 'I weren't frightened.' The evidence Ivy provides for this is that she would 'show off' or 'have a right go' in situations where people were talking about Fiona. After the incident recounted above when two women upset Fiona by talking about her unwed status, Ivy had Fiona moved to a different ward. To us this is supportive evidence of the initial link between agoraphobia and Fiona's pregnancy: further defensive reactions against the anxiety of her daughter's status as a young unmarried mother. Another piece of evidence supporting our interpretation is that Jonathan's illegitimate status is even now routinely evaded by the fact that, at least to us, he is referred to as a brother by Kelly and Tommy.

According to psychoanalytic theory, such symptoms as agoraphobia express a deeply felt contradiction which cannot be rendered conscious because it is extremely anxiety-provoking. In our interpretation, by becoming agoraphobic, Ivy was able to avoid exposing herself to the shame that would result from being talked about by neighbours who, she imagined, were criticising the family for their lack of respectability in having a young unmarried pregnant daughter.

We also know, from a mixture of sociological knowledge and the cultural knowledge shared between interviewee and researcher, that in 1960s England illegitimacy was the antithesis of respectability and that this stigma would have attached to the family. As we have seen in Tommy's case, investment in a respectable identity can be all the more important if you are from a big, 'rough', working-class family. However, the criteria are gendered: for women, respectability means sexual respectability. Ivy's daughter Kelly makes it clear how her mother's preoccupation with her daughters' respectability had a profound effect on her as a teenager.

Kelly is the youngest of the three daughters and the only one to marry before becoming pregnant. In response to a general question from Wendy about things earlier in her life that worried her, she does not hesitate in coming out with three issues which turn out to be inseparable:

> *Kelly:* I think I've always worried about things. I've worried about boyfriends, er, I've worried about what me mum thinks. Er, I worried about becoming pregnant early … Wo-wo-worried about boyfriends because er, like … er, I'd got – got two sisters … who'd got pregnant quite early. My sister were married at 16 and my other sister were like 14 when she were pregnant and 15 when she 'ad 'er baby … And I can remember 'aving a kiss with someone and I were worried sick that I were 'aving a baby … there were no sex involved at 'ome or anythin'. [*Wendy:* Yeah.] Er, never saw any sex or any cuddles with my dad at that time, what I can remember of 'im, er, so sex were a dirty word to me mother.

In consequence, Kelly remained a virgin until marriage at 18, and symbolised this with a white wedding:

> *Kelly:* I got married in white and that were me virginity, and I lost it when I – on me wedding night … and that were because my mum 'ad dug it into me 'ead that much, because my other two sisters 'ad let me mum down and shamed 'er, as it were called, shamed and God knows what else.

In this passage, Kelly makes a firm connection between the signficance of her white (virgin) wedding as the opposite of the shame wrought on Ivy by Kelly's two older sisters.

Let us summarise the information that has so far contributed to making the link that has solved the puzzle of Ivy's agoraphobia and then make the interpretation that is supported by it. After that we will go on to build the picture between such links and the *Gestalt*. We have gathered together:

- information provided in the text (for example, Ivy's agoraphobia, Fiona's pregnancy at 14; Kelly's account of her mother's feelings about sex);
- a free association by Ivy linking two pieces of information (Fiona's pregnancy and not going out for fear that the neighbours would talk);
- shared cultural assumptions of interviewee and researcher (the significance of a 'white' wedding; the 'shame' of illegitimacy in 1960s England);
- sociological knowledge (the class connotations and gender differences in respectability in a family such as the Walters);
- psychoanalytic knowledge (agoraphobia expressing unconscious conflict).

As a result, we can come up with an interpretation that, by being stricken with agoraphobia, Ivy achieved the result of not having to expose herself to the shame of being talked about by neighbours who, she expected, were maligning the family for their lack of respectability in having an unmarried pregnant daughter. This understanding of Ivy is psychosocial because it shows her being positioned in a contemporary discourse concerning respectability, but it escapes the potential determinism of that analysis by showing how she negotiated and resisted this through the inner conflicts which it precipitated. In Ivy's case (because of the way in which the social meaning of respectability was inserted in her biography, see below) she dealt with the conflict with a symptom of whose origins she remained unaware. In this sense, her response was psychosocial.

From single to multiple links

We now have a psychosocial proposition about Ivy, namely that her own identity is invested in respectability. If this is so, it will cast light on other information in the text, imbuing significance into parts of her account and making new links. For this purpose, we will use the example of Ivy's admission that she and Albert were never married, an admission that she purposely introduced during the second interview:

> *Ivy:* I've never been married me, you know.
> *Wendy:* Aha. I didn't know.
> *Ivy:* I meant telling ya last week. No. I got in with Albert when I were 18. And I stopped – 'e's the only man I've ever 'ad. And they didn't like it, me mum and dad, because I weren't married.[17] But I changed me name

by deed ... I 'ad it all changed and all me kids is in Walters and I'm in Walters. But I weren't bothered about that, we were 'appy. And 'e were good. But the trouble was, 'e was already married ... And 'e never 'ad any children to 'er. And I 'ad nine to 'im didn't I? But I don't regret it, don't get me wrong. But no I've never, ever been married. And I'm not ashamed on it.

Furnished with the proposition that Ivy is invested in sexual respectability for her daughters, this extract is rich with significance. She had upset her parents' ideas of respectability by having a sexual relationship with a married man (who was also 15 years older), in a parallel way to Fiona's later behaviour. At 18 she stopped. Whatever it was she stopped doing, she censors the telling of it to the interviewer. One possible meaning is that she then stopped (stayed) with Albert. Alternatively, the association with what comes next could suggest that what she stopped doing was going with other men. We have no further evidence of the possibility that she was having sex with them, a possibility which she is quick to contradict by her claim that Albert is 'the only man I've ever 'ad' (an oft-repeated claim). Given her worries about sexual respectability, it would be likely that she would claim this whatever the truth of her early sexual behaviour. It is not clear at what point she became pregnant with her first child; whether he was still living with his wife, for example. This might easily explain their decision to live together.

The act of changing her name by deed poll to his name enabled her in effect to masquerade as married from then on. We learned elsewhere that only the two eldest children knew this secret, right up until Albert died. Here, as in many other places in the transcripts, she emphasises what a good husband Albert was. She claims that she 'weren't bothered', 'don't regret it' and is 'not ashamed on it', all in the space of a few sentences (and again elsewhere), yet the fact that it was secret appears to contradict the idea that she wasn't ashamed. This interpretation is supported by our initial proposition about Ivy's concern with sexual respectability for her daughters.

We also found examples in the text which suggest that this still concerns her. Since her husband died when she was 49, she has not entered into another relationship, a fact which she repeats with pride, but no hint of regret: ' 'e were a good 'un. I've never 'ad anybody since. Nobody can come and do that on me, and that's a lot to say.' In this claim, Ivy's pride appears to be linked to the fact that nobody could accuse her of unrespectable sexual behaviour.

With the above information, we can confidently add the proposition that Ivy was concerned for her own sexual respectability. We have established two interrelated themes at this point: Ivy's own emotional involvement in her daughters' sexual respectability, and in her own. These are two generalisations which have been made on the basis of evidence, theory and interpretation. If it is possible to theorise a link between them, we will have made a further advance in understanding the form of Ivy's 'whole'. Clearly, sexual respectability constitutes the link at the level of social theory: values that impinged on Ivy in the 1940s had not completely died out in the 1960s, when Sally and Fiona got pregnant. However, this does not account for Ivy's uncommonly strong response – a breakdown and a subsequent lifetime of agoraphobia. If we suppose that the strength of her response was related to the way that her own unresolved status with Albert was being relived through identifying with her daughters' respectability, we find some evidence for this. For example, Ivy described the compulsiveness with which she was involved with Fiona's pregnancy and birth: 'I couldn't keep away. I 'ad to be there all the time.' This is quite opposite to a common reaction of the time in which mothers disowned their daughters when they were pregnant and kept a distance from the event. We don't know how Ivy's mother was with Ivy's illegitimate babies, only that Ivy's mother (still alive at over 90) refuses to speak to her, and another sister, now.

There is further evidence for Ivy's identification with Fiona.[18] When Fiona was young, even after having the baby, she liked to go out and 'fly 'er kite'. Ivy used to be out 'seven nights a week'. When Ivy described how Fiona got into fights (two convictions for grievous bodily harm), she likened her daughter to herself: 'I were a fighter.' They had almost the same number of children (unmarried) and they were both mothers to Jonathan. The relationship was full of difficulty and Ivy returned to it many times during the interview, acknowledging some guilt about what she had done to Fiona by rejecting her as a baby and subsequently.

On the issue of sexual respectability, however, Ivy's own identifications appear to dictate that she stick up for Fiona, the reprobate daughter. Fiona has her sexuality exonerated by Ivy with the words 'But I can honestly say this, she only 'ad ... our Jonathan to that lad and she's only 'ad Denny for 'er other seven children. She's 'ad nobody else since.' In contrast, Kelly, the only one to have had a white wedding and who is now ensconced in a respectable marriage, occupies in her mother's fantasy the position of having ' 'ad some men, don't you worry' (the tone conveyed a prurient interest which is not consistent with criticism by a mother who believes in monogamy). This paradox may be explained by Ivy's envy of the daughter who has achieved respectability and (in Ivy's fantasy) wider sexual experience. It is powerful evidence of a defensive splitting of these two daughters with respect to their sexual respectability. Once we have established this, we can, as in the case of Tommy above, use this theoretical tool to cast light on other aspects of Ivy's relationships; for example, her idealisation of husband Albert and of eldest daughter Sally. The point has we hope been made.

In the above passages, we have been tracing a series of links, each one informed by the wider significance we had built up about Ivy's relationship to sexual respectability. We have traced these quite formally for the purposes of explication. However, the way in which they actually happened is better described by the ideas of intuition and sudden insight (interspersed with a lot of hard work), rather than the formal logical process which is represented here. Either way, we have tried to illustrate how the form of a person's account is the sum of all the links that have been made (and can be made) within the available material. The first link was low level; other links were between whole groups of evidence brought together by propositions concerning sexual respectability. The links were characterised by both social and psychological explanations, in this way fulfilling our claim to represent psychosocial subjects.

Our theory, clinical psychoanalysis and 'scientific' knowledge

It is obvious that our research is deeply indebted to psychoanalysis, both theoretically and methodologically: our subject is one that is not only positioned within the surrounding social discourses, but motivated by unconscious investments and defences against anxiety; our data production is based on the principle of free association; and our data analysis depends on interpretation. In this section, we want, first, to discuss the relationship between principles of interpretation which have largely been developed in a clinical psychoanalytic setting, where the purpose is therapeutic, and those relevant to a research setting; and, secondly, how these match up against the main criteria adopted by science, namely objectivity and reliability.

There is a huge literature on interpretation as therapeutic technique: for a long time the interpretation was considered as the single method whereby an analyst could alleviate the mental distress of a patient by making the unconscious conscious (Sandler, et al., 1990: Ch. 10). It is useful to be able to have access to the store of experience, theory and critique that has been generated by clinical psychoanalysts concerning their use of interpretation, but the differences between that setting and our research setting need to be specified so that we do not overgeneralise its applicability.

The primary difference between the two practices is that clinicians interpret *into* the encounter, whereas researchers will save their interpretations for outside it. Put another way, researchers, not being therapists, will be careful not to interpret at the time the information is being provided by interviewees. Their interpretative work comes later, is separate from the participant and has a different audience. Research interpretation is therefore an activity associated with data analysis as opposed to data production. However, this distinction breaks down in the necessary exchanges of understanding taking place in the interview. In the earlier extract, when Wendy, the interviewer, asks 'Is that one of the reasons you didn't like to go out?' it is, in effect, an interpretation formulated as a question. Its effect, as we saw, was to mobilise Ivy's defences. However, these were informative.

The second major difference is that the object of clinical psychoanalysis is the individual person (sometimes a couple or small group). Even if an analyst has an appreciation of the social circumstances that have helped to create the patient, he or she has a responsibility to assist that individual's change. In practice, this has tended to mean that psychoanalytic theory has emphasised the inner world (and the intersubjective one) rather than the social, external world. In using psychoanalytic methodology as part of understanding a psychosocial subject, we have illustrated above how, with regard to respect and respectability, it is possible to broaden the reach of interpretation.[19] We now need to see how compatible our approach to interpretation is with the scientific method.

Objectivity

Objectivity is a contentious principle in contemporary social science. A positivist epistemology (theory of knowledge), strictly applied, is based on the belief that knowledge can be secured through demonstrating its direct correspondence with observed events. Objectivity and reliability are two principles through which this goal is pursued. Qualitative research has parted company to varying degrees with these principles, depending on its theory of knowledge (Madill et al., 2000). The questioning of the possibility of objectivity in clinical psychoanalysis goes back much further because the nature of clinical work forced psychoanalysts to theorise the role of the analyst in the meanings that were circulating in the analytic space (Heimann, 1950). Psychoanalysis has largely conceded that interpretation is an art and not a science and therefore psychoanalysts have been prepared to theorise issues like intuition, use of the analyst's subjectivity, the role of emotion in thinking and the use of unconscious dynamics as a tool for knowledge. At the same time, analysts have grappled with the issue of how not to impose false or bad interpretations on their patients. This has resulted in a tolerance for paradox and uncertainty which can usefully be borrowed. For example, when Schwaber insists that another person's subjectivity can only be known through one's own, he continues with an argument for 'vigilantly guarding against the imposition of the analyst's point of view' (quoted in Aron, 1996: 54). Likewise Smith, 'while acknowledging that "actual neutrality is a fiction", does not conclude that neutrality should be abandoned, [but rather] "the less possible it is to be neutral in fact, the more crucial it is to strive towards it"' (quoted in Aron, 1996: 107).

It is through the acknowledgement of such tensions that psychoanalysis has paid increasing attention to the principle of unconscious intersubjectivity (for example, the gradual development of the idea of countertransference; see Hinshelwood, 1991). As in social science, the original tendency was to see the analyst as an external, quasi-objective agent who worked on the patient's material. Now the unconscious intersubjective dynamics between patient and analyst is increasingly regarded as a central means of understanding and helping the patient. While this is not appropriate for every methodology nor every subject area in social science, the same principle applies wherever the nature of the research requires an understanding of the meanings through which research subjects communicate information to researchers. Psychoanalytic approaches to research reflect this view: 'the psychoanalytic exploration of fieldwork pays particular attention to ... how unconscious processes structure relations between researcher, subject and the data gathered' (Hunt, 1989: 9). The same applies to interviewing.

For a social science still imbued with positivist principles about objectivity, fact and replicable evidence, the principle of unconscious intersubjectivity generates huge doubts about the validity of the knowledge generated. Unlike clinicians, we cannot refer to the promotion of the patient's development as a criterion (Bion, 1984: iii) (difficult though that is to evaluate). One useful summary of the rules for evidence (in qualitative clinical research) is that the stories told by researchers must be 'methodologically, rhetorically and clinically convincing' (Miller and Crabtree, 1994: 348).

Reliability

Reliability refers to the consistency, stability and repeatability of results (Brink, 1991, cited in Madill et al., 2000). However, this definition assumes that meanings can be controlled and made identical in successive applications of a question. It is therefore an invalid criterion in our theoretical view: meanings are unique as well as shared. Contrary to the view of positivist science, however, the situations that we are analysing are never replicable (were they ever?). Meanings are not just unique to a person (although more or less shared as well); they are also unique to a relational encounter (though, again paradoxically, partly consistent over time as well). The main plank of our defence of the knowledge we generate using interpretation is in the notion of evidence. Our work, as well as being theoretically led, is solidly empirical in the sense that supporting and challenging evidence is available. We have demonstrated this in our step-by-step analyses of Tommy and Ivy, above. For example, time and again there is evidence of what we have interpreted as Tommy's defensive idealisation. This makes our interpretation 'robust', a notion we have borrowed from scientific methodology. The principles of interpretative data analysis that we have set out in this chapter can be tested in the sense that they can be applied to different data, by different researchers who can assess their utility in casting light on narrative accounts. Their reliability can be checked (though never guaranteed) if, when our interpretations and analyses are studied by others,[20] they are 'recognised'; that is, the sense that we made out of them can be shared through the subjectivity of others (including you, the reader). This does not rule out the possibility of alternative explanations, but these too can be tested against the available data. If you, the reader, wish to offer a different interpretation of our data, you are welcome to do so.

We have now considered both the distinctive theoretical and methodological issues raised for the production and analysis of data with defended, psychosocial subjects. Does such a starting-point have similarly distinctive ethical implications? It is to this question that we turn in the next chapter.

Summary

- Tommy's relationship to his childhood was discussed in relation to 'common-sense', the whole, theory and reflexivity.
- By using all the available evidence, our psychosocial theory and the reflexivity of the interviewer, we were able to explain otherwise contradictory material, the kind overlooked by researchers committed to giving voice to their interviewees.
- Our theoretical commitment to holistic interpretation was contrasted with the widespread tendency to fragment data in the interests of systematic coding.
- We described the use of structured summaries and pen portraits as aids to holistic analysis and traced the analytical process which enabled a holistic interpretation of Ivy's relationship to sexual respectability.
- We concluded by discussing how to apply criteria such as objectivity and reliability to interpretations of research data informed by clinical psychoanalysis.

Notes

1 For the purposes of this chapter, which is methodologically orientated, we are not analysing this extract with a particular research question in mind, but going back to more preliminary questions of technique with regard to analysing qualitative data.

2 By whole we do not imply 'total'. Rather, we wish to emphasise the importance of holding on to all of the accumulated data or material when interpreting a part, both that produced by the interviewee and that which such material sparks off in the interviewer. New material or a different interviewer could lead to the production of further links or new *Gestalts*.

3 Since we know that Ivy tended to portray things in extremes, it helps us to be cautious about her factual claims: 'never stopping in once' might just mean going out frequently.

4 Though we hope our notion of the psychosocial defended subject is clear by now, it is important that you, the reader, remember (a) not to confuse it with traditional Freudian psychoanalysis since it owes more to post-Freudian developments, especially those inspired by the work of Melanie Klein, and their stress on intersubjectivity; and (b) to hang on to the other link to the social, the one inspired pre-eminently by the work of Foucault with its emphasis on power/knowledge/discourse (see Henriques et al., 1998).

5 This was for Jonathan, the child of her older sister, Fiona, who was taken into the family when Fiona was regarded as incapable of taking care of him herself. He was called a 'brother' by Ivy and Albert's children, though in fact he was a nephew.

6 Similarly, his neighbour Sean, a friend since schooldays, remains 'a smashing lad' despite a whole host of anti-social and criminal behaviour which Tommy catalogued: in his case, being 'ignorant' excused him (see Hollway and Jefferson, 1999).

7 We use the example of the respectable working-class man, not just because we wish to talk about Tommy, but also because the original idea of the respectable working classes, being blind to issues of gender, assumed men as the benchmark.

8 We should also note Tommy's clear preference for the term 'respect' in what follows; in discursive terms, his investment in being positioned as 'respected' (not 'respectable').

9 We note in passing that the extract is littered once again with Tommy's characteristic tendency to idealise his childhood, as evidenced in words like 'fantastic', 'brilliant' and 'unbelievable'.

10 Given the very different biographical trajectories of Tommy and me (Tony), I found it hard at first to reconcile the idea of 'being known' with 'respect'. I felt that it was a depleted notion of respect. This seems to be an example of a countertransference blinding me to Tommy's world, but which Wendy was able to notice. This is an example of the use of triangulation of our two perspectives on the data.

11 A subjective perspective provides the kind of emotional involvement which could lead to distortions but, if it is recognised and used systematically, provides a further dimension of information. As Schwaber (in Aron, 1996: 57) says, 'we can discover another's subjectivity only by using our own.'

12 These links can now be made not only between elements coded by the same category and between categories, but also by linking data categories with higher-order conceptual categories (Richards and Richards, 1994).

13 This term is used by Miller and Crabtree to describe one of four 'idealized analytic styles' (1994: 345) on a continuum representing different distances in the relationship between the analyst and the text.

14 For Bion, unlike Freud's theory of wish fulfilment, the function of dreaming was to synthesise elements into a whole (Symington and Symington, 1996: 7).

15   Projective identification is 'a process by which the infant's thoughts that cannot be thought and feelings that cannot be felt are elicited in the mother when the mother is able to make herself psychologically available to be used in this way' (Ogden, 1994: 44). The parallel capacity between analyst and patient have been much evidenced in the clinical literature and it is argued that this capacity for unconscious communication is more general.

16   This is in marked contrast to some usage in narrative analysis. For example, Linde whose book on life stories is subtitled 'The Creation of Coherence', argues that inconsistencies in an interviewee's narrative should lead the researcher to go back for a 'meta account' (1993: 34). In effect the researcher is challenging them and trying to get an account beyond inconsistency. According to Linde, her interviewees were so discomforted by this attempt that she abandoned it on ethical grounds. To us, this example illustrates how a method can create coherence and then impose it on a theory of the subject.

17   Ivy's father treated his wife very badly, often violently, and also some of his children, including Ivy: 'We 'ad a shocking life at 'ome with my dad.' She was thrown out of home by him at 16. At 33 to her 18, Albert must have felt a bit like the good father to her:' 'e were good bloke, 'e were a good 'un.'

18   Such evidence is in line with the literature on mother–daughter relations which suggests that some daughters have difficulty psychologically separating from their mothers and vice versa (Ernst, 1997).

19   Despite these differences, we should not lose sight of what is common to both forms of interpretation, namely, 'the art of understanding the unconscious meaning of the patient's material' [in our case, 'research participant's'] (Sandler et al., 1990: 107).

20   Our data (in the form of discs, not audiotapes, to protect anonymity) are publicly available through Qualidata, the ESRC-funded project to make available qualitative data for study and secondary analysis. Qualidata is based at the University of Essex, Department of Sociology.

CHAPTER 5

THE ETHICS OF RESEARCHING PSYCHOSOCIAL SUBJECTS

Our purpose in this chapter is to discuss guidelines and debates about ethical research practice in the light of our propositions about the research subject. Specifically, we shall address the following questions:

- are the available guidelines appropriate?
- what implications for ethics follow from positing a psychosocial subject, specifically one who deploys unconscious defences against anxiety?
- what ethical principles would be appropriate given the methods we have developed for producing and analysing data with such subjects?

We use three contrasting case examples for this purpose, based both on our psychosocial model of the subject and the interpretations of evidence which derive from it. The first two are from our research on anxiety and the fear of crime, which is by now familiar to you. Here, we discuss ethical issues relating to both data production and data analysis. The third is our analysis of newspaper reports of a criminal trial of a 'date-rape' allegation (Hollway and Jefferson, 1998). The publicly available nature of the information and the potential for identification of the two students involved posed us with a further set of ethical dilemmas. We end by summarising what for us are the appropriate principles for researching psychosocial subjects.

Ethical issues in social-science research are concerned to 'ensure that the interests of participants in research are safeguarded' (British Psychological Society, 1996: 1). Under 'interests' issues of both rights and welfare are subsumed. Until relatively recently, such issues were not taken very seriously when weighed in the balance against the interests of science in advancing knowledge. Now, ethical guidelines in, for example, medicine, sociology and psychology provide specific guidance for researchers, who are often required to get clearance from ethics committees before proceeding with a piece of research.

Such guidelines commonly begin with a general statement which talks in terms of principles such as 'they shall value integrity, impartiality and respect for persons and evidence' (British Psychological Society, 1996: 1) and 'members have a responsibility both to safeguard the proper interests of those involved in or affected by their work, and to report their findings accurately and truthfully' (British Sociological

Association, 1996: 1). In applying these principles to our research into the fear of crime, how were we to define them in our research practice? How can such principles operate when the field of research is by definition discomforting, when researchers want to know about fear and anxiety, threats to the self and the painful emotions to do with love and loss, dependency and desire? How can participants be ethically engaged to consider such topics?

Payment and power

There were two noteworthy aspects concerning the prior information on which our interviewees' consent was initially based. First, the payment and its timing and, secondly, the generality of the information. This section explores the issues of payment and power; the following section the question of informed consent.

During the initial doorstep meeting at which we invited people to participate in our research, we told each participant that we would pay a 'small fee – £15 – at the end of the second interview'. By paying them for their time, we may variously have been experienced as equalising the relationship (our money for their time) or as having the material power that the financial relation afforded us. Payment can be seen as a means of inducement which undermines the free choice of a person to participate in research. We took the first view: namely that, for people who were often unemployed or at least very hard up, remuneration for their time was important, and a mark of our respect for their participation. The timing of payment at the end of the second interview may have induced people to continue when otherwise they would have wished to withdraw. Two people withdrew after the first interview: one man who turned out to have Alzheimer's disease, who was withdrawn by a relative, and one woman whose life seemed too chaotic to adhere to any prearranged time and place.

It was in our interests to get two interviews with as many of our participants as possible. An understanding of interests should be accompanied by a consideration of power, since interests are accomplished through the exercise of power. Power, in the sense of 'ability to do something' or 'capacity of producing some effect' (*Shorter Oxford English Dictionary*), always involves an ethical dimension. Power is most commonly assessed in terms of structural disparities between members of social groups. In our case, our status as university researchers (educated, employed and middle class) differentiated us from those we were interviewing. Ethical guidelines are often based on scenarios of unequal power, especially scenarios where researchers could abuse their superior power in situations in which participants may not be in a position to protect themselves.[1] However, we were on their territory and depended on their hospitality and cooperation.

Working in the context of such power differences was inevitable and it was useful to understand power also in more relational, dynamic and positive ways. The structural understanding of power implies that power can be equalised out – for example, by having people of the same social status as interviewers. A post-structuralist understanding sees power as inherent in all social relations (however equalised) and balances the structuralist tendency to see power as harmful with a view of the 'positivity' of power; that is, its capacity to produce things. Structural differences like education might have led participants to assume that we knew better than them, and in consequence they may have been loath to challenge, disagree with or dissent from our definition of the situation. On the other hand, the tendency of participants to see us as very knowledgeable meant that when we did understand, sympathise and recognise their dilemmas, it could have a powerful emotional effect. Likewise, if we were not upset or disconcerted by some admission, it could begin to feel less disconcerting or upsetting to them (that is, we would 'contain' it).

These examples illustrate that we are interested in how relational dynamics, such as understanding and respect, has the capacity to transcend structural power differences. Such relational dynamics, which draws on the deep pool of common human characteristics, does not equalise power, but it makes it negotiable, rather than an inevitable effect of status differences. It shifts the emphasis from the exercise of power *per se* to its effects in context.

Informed consent and harm: the case of Fran

The second aspect of our information was its generality. We had a prompt sheet for our introductory information which started 'We are researchers attached to the University of …'. Then we gave the following general statement about the research: 'We are conducting research into people's feelings about crime, about risk, and generally about safety and we are interested in people's experiences in these sorts of areas.' We did not want to constrain the topic by defining it narrowly, thus encouraging people to tailor their information to what they assumed we wanted. Especially, we did not want to frame our research questions in such a way that people's understanding of what we wanted were arguments, opinions or explanations because this would be contrary to our commitment to the principles of narrative interviewing and free association.

Our formulation was therefore very open and expressly did not specify what ideas we were wanting to test out; for example, whether the fear of crime acted as a vehicle for expressing other, less controllable anxieties. In our view it is important to make a clear distinction between the questions that the research is asking, formulated in the academic domain, and information and explanations that we provide to interviewees. This is because it is important not to prejudice the research by signalling, in the framing of the information, the researcher's expectations. Where this is done, researchers may get the answers that they already have in mind, and common or dominant discourses do not get challenged and disrupted. In framing our introductory information in such a general manner, we were led by the interests of the research, but we could think of no good reason why it was contrary to participants' interests: it was clear, non-technical and open enough for them to engage with in ways that interested them.

We were also aware of a more intractable issue concerning informed consent.[2] We felt that it was impossible to inform participants in advance, in ways that would be meaningful, about the experience of our kind of interviews. Their experience of researchers (if any) was based on market and survey researchers who would ask structured questions and tick boxes on forms. The questions would be about specific behaviours or opinions. Often, the moment we broached our subject matter, people would volunteer their opinions about crime in the locality. It was only through the experience of the first interview that they would come to realise what telling stories about their experiences to people like us could entail. Fran exemplifies the complexity of the ethics of consent.

Fran was a 35-year-old woman, separated from her husband, who had been living with her two children on the low-crime council housing estate for less than a year. She quickly accepted to be interviewed when we knocked on her back door and introduced ourselves and the research. She came across as sure about wanting to participate, but I (Wendy) noted her manner as being closed or cold. At the beginning of the first interview she was quite brusque and instrumental about it. She noticeably eased up as we proceeded. After the tape was turned off at the end of the first interview, she commented on how she had 'opened up' to me (Wendy), a stranger, after what she'd said about being suspicious of strangers. She seemed to enjoy this idea.

By the end of the second interview, she had talked, among other things, about her relationships with her ex-husband and with her children, a childhood characterised by a violent father (who assaulted her brother not her) and her fear of rape and sexual assault (see Chapter 6 for a brief discussion). These topics involved some risk of psychological distress in the sense that her sense of self was inseparable from them and they were not all pleasant topics. The criterion of avoiding harm is a basic ethical principle: inflicting harm is unethical and contrary to rights and welfare. However, is it necessarily harmful to experience being upset or distressed? It can be reassuring and therapeutic to talk about an upsetting event in a safe context.

In our following discussions, we want to shift the emphasis away from ethical principles which tend to treat distress and harm as equivalent problems by theorising the relational context in which distress may be experienced. The conflation of harm and distress tends towards an ethical principle that participants should be left unchanged by their experience of the research (which is anyway impossible).[3] Perhaps the decisive ethical difference is that in our research context participants are active co-participants in the relationship within which the interview data are produced (see, for example, Mishler, 1986; for a critique, Scheurich, 1997).

While it is true that Fran was actively involved in talking about private and intimate topics, she had not anticipated it. This was made clear by a question she asked at the end of the second interview, in response to a 'debriefing' question:

Wendy: Is there anything else you'd like to ask?
Fran: Er well what we've talked about, things like my past and me dad and my relationship now, and when I met [her ex-husband] … and everything. How does this come into it [the research]?

As with Jane (see Chapter 3), I explained about the principles of the research that made these areas relevant. Fran's later comment (once the tape was turned off) suggested that she was not discomforted: she commented that she thought she would like to go and get some counselling after all (an option she had considered and rejected a while back). I understood her to mean that she now had experience of the value of talking about personal, emotionally difficult issues in a supportive and trustworthy context. To be more precise, the interview provided the context of a relationship with someone who was capable of listening well (especially paying attention to emotional significances), was not competing for attention, who could reflect back in questions and comments a recognition of her experiences which was emotionally appropriate, and by whom she did not feel judged. These are the characteristics of a good counselling relationship. But they are also very effective in eliciting the kind of information that we require for our kind of research – information which goes beyond rationalisation and opinion, which conveys emotional significance and does not avoid potentially distressing issues.

There was no way of conveying in advance that Fran might disclose this kind of material.[4] Indeed, there was no way of predicting if she would or not. For example, we had a rather unsatisfactory couple of interviews with an older man, whom we called Joseph, who remained fairly uninformative throughout, answering questions briefly and factually and not telling many stories. His life remained an enigma to us, not least because there were so many features of it that were unusual and begged many questions. We will never know whether Joseph was keeping a great deal from us, although we suspect he was. What is relevant for ethical considerations is that we can assume that he did not reveal what would have been uncomfortable for him to reveal; that is, his defences worked to protect himself from unwanted intrusion.

To construe this as a 'choice' or a 'decision' is slightly misleading since it does not have to be the case that Joseph or Fran was aware, either in advance or during the interview, that he or she would or would not reveal certain information. It seems more appropriate to construe the 'choice' to reveal something as part of a continuing dynamic between two people. Questions concerning trust and respect are constantly at issue and at any moment can change the direction of what is said and the meanings that are exchanged.

The decision to consent, then, cannot be reduced to a conscious, cognitive process but is a continuing emotional awareness that characterises every interaction. In our view, it is based on a very different theory about how people process information than the one on which the idea of informed consent is based, which emphasises people's capacities to process information and reach a rational and considered decision as an autonomous subject, sealed off from the influences of others. It assumes that a person is in a better position to judge prior to the interaction with the researcher (prior, we might point out, to the evidence on which trust is largely based). Our impression of people's doorstep decisions was that these had less to do with the information we offered them, although that was an important baseline, and more to do with their feelings about us. Such feelings would be a mixture of the impressions that we were actually conveying and the fantasies that people had about two strangers like us walking around their neighbourhood. (Someone told us later that they had thought, at first sight, that we were Jehovah's Witnesses; someone else, local journalists.) We had greater success when as a couple we knocked on doors asking for access than if either of us was alone.

Fran's example suggests to us that the central criterion on which the ethics of participation in this kind of research should be based should not be *informed* consent (though preliminary consent must, of course, be sought based on some information). Rather, it should revolve around the criterion of guarding against harm. In the depth psychological realm that concerns us, assessing harm is neither simple nor completely predictable. We put the emphasis on the researcher's responsibility for creating a safe context, in which issues of honesty, sympathy and respect were central (to which we return below).[5] If we had decided upon an ethics which involved forewarning Fran about the possibility of discussing intimate issues, our guess is that she would have backed off, which was not in the interests of our research.[6]

If this suggests a lack of properly informed consent, it also suggests that the more appropriate criterion in Fran's case was the consequences of her consenting. We do not know whether she pursued the option of counselling or – if she did – whether it was beneficial. But we are fairly confident that the research experience was a positive one. It might be objected that it was helpful for Fran, but what about others, who had a less positive experience? Our point is twofold. First, the conduct of the interview can go a long way to ensuring that it will not be a negative experience. Secondly, if interviewees do not feel positive about the relationship, this – particularly if it is respected by the interviewer – will serve to limit what they disclose of themselves.

The BSA suggests that 'it may be necessary for the obtaining of consent to be regarded, not as a once-for-all prior event, but as a process subject to renegotiation over time' (BSA, 1996: 2). Our understanding of the process is even more continuous than this. Typically, the guidelines construe the issue of consent as 'before' and 'after' the research intervention. 'After', for them, involves 'debriefing' to deal with ethical issues which arise from discrepancies between prior information and fuller information which, by implication, it is the right of participants to know at the end. If certain information has been withheld in the interests of a valid study, the guidance suggests that 'full information' should be provided retrospectively about 'the aims, rationale and outcomes of the process as far as it is consistent with a concern for the welfare of the participants' (BPS, 1996: 2). Debriefing involves providing 'the participants with any necessary information to complete their understanding of the nature of the research' and discussing 'their experience of the research in order to monitor any unforeseen negative effects or misconceptions' (BPS, 1996: 9). For the BPS, the central principle in deciding whether research which is dependent upon deception is acceptable to conduct is 'the reaction of participants when deception was revealed. If this led to discomfort, anger or objections from the participants then the deception was inappropriate' (1996: 5).

We are not talking about deception here, although we have to keep in view that there may be a conflict of interests involved between our wish to keep the interview terrain as open as possible and participants' early expectations that they will talk specifically about 'crime, risk and safety'. To the extent that the BPS criterion of participants' reactions is relevant, Fran's comment about getting counselling can be taken as evidence of a positive experience. If we then apply the primary ethical principle of well-being (or, put less strongly, avoidance of harm), we can sum up the issue in Fran's case as follows. Some emotional upset would be a likely consequence of confronting the real, but painful issues she was facing in her life at a time of transition. Although raising these was not the purpose of the research, if she found herself doing so because it felt like a good place to do so, then the outcome would be consistent with her well-being or welfare. However, just in case it is beginning to sound as if people can be single-minded about such 'choices',[7] it is worth pointing out that Fran probably felt ambivalent about her disclosures. This would be the implication of a model of subjectivity based on conflict and ambivalence, rather than certainty.

Confidentiality: the case of the Walters family

The example of the Walters family raises a series of ethical issues concerning confidentiality. Confidentiality can be one of the least problematic of the ethical issues. If information is treated and used in such a way as to be secure and to ensure the anonymity of participants, the ethical responsibility usually ends there. This should be the case 'whether or not an explicit pledge of confidentiality has been given' (BSA, 1996: 2). However, as biographical methods become more commonplace in social research, questions about anonymity, about the feasibility of concealing a person's identity in published research, take on a new complexity: 'potential informants and research participants, especially those possessing a combination of attributes which make them readily identifiable, may need to be reminded that it can be difficult to disguise their identity without introducing an unacceptably large measure of distortion into the data' (BSA, 1996: 3). The more detailed the case study, and the more it draws on psychological, rather than just social, principles, the harder it is to protect a person's anonymity in publicly available work. The vast majority of people would not know, and could not recognise, our participants. However a family member, close friend or the person themselves could hardly fail to do so, no matter how many superficial details were changed (as we have done).

The production and use of data from several members of the same family make further ethical demands (the same principle could well apply to members of the same neighbourhood or organisation who knew each other). Irrespective of what we negotiated with any one of the Walters family, we had a responsibility not to convey to one what we had learned about him or her from another. This duty was quite salient in a family characterised by dislike and discord among the three we interviewed. It did not just rule out questions or comments explicitly relating to what another had said, but even using knowledge in the form of questions or understandings which we might have derived from another family member.

The responsibility to preserve confidentiality has clear consequences for decisions to make data available to respondents. Following earlier humanistic and feminist critiques of the potential of research for exploiting participants (Reason and Rowan, 1981; Roberts, 1982), researchers advocated that the products of research should be fed back into the group or community from which the data derived. Others have pointed out the difficulties and compromises that this can entail (Olesen, 1994). This is based on the principle of accountability of researchers to those whose lives they claim to understand. Whether it is meaningful, or in a single participant's interest, to show him or her an analysis based on his or her single case is debatable (see below). Where analysis is based on several people, the answer is clear cut: showing anybody an analysis based on someone they are likely to recognise would be contrary to undertakings of confidentiality. For example, if Tommy tells Kelly to her face what he told us about hating his sister (see Chapter 4) that is not our business, but it is our responsibility that Kelly does not find this out through us. If the case study is published in any form, we can never be entirely sure that this will not happen. Will one of the Walters come across this book? It is unlikely but not impossible. Since the only resolution that would guarantee that this could not happen would be not to publish case-based studies, there is a profound conflict of interests between participant confidentiality and the wider interest in publicly available knowledge. We have not resolved this conflict, only decided that publication is warranted (for reasons we expand upon in the next section).

There has been a different debate about the control that researchers might feel responsible for exercising over the use of their research (Alderson, 1998; Hood-Williams and Harrison, 1998). This has been focused by the new availability of qualitative data for secondary analysis through Qualidata (the ESRC Qualitative Data Archival Resource Centre). Alderson (1998) expressed her worries that later analysts might use her data in ways that she or the participants might disapprove of or regret. Hood-Williams and Harrison (1998) argued that her concerns could be applied equally to primary and secondary analyses since the researcher does not control subsequent interpretations of published work, whether primary or secondary, nor 'the uses to which a piece of research may be put' (1998: 8). The idea that published research can be controlled depends on an idea of language as capable of meaning only what its creator intended. Current models of language emphasise the multiple meanings that it will generate in its various uses.

We have lodged our transcripts with Qualidata, taking two sets of measures to preserve anonymity. First, we have not made audiotapes available. Secondly, we have been assured that identifying details such as names and locations are erased from the publicly available record. Beyond that, we believe that we are not in a position to control how these data are used by others. Moreover, our purposes in our own use of the data do not ensure that they will be received in the intended manner: 'the transformations which take place to the primary material in the course of research are themselves potentially problematic ... the research can blossom into intensely intimate and belief-changing processes; but it might also leave the respondents unable to recognise their words or thoughts in the reported findings' (Hood-Williams and Harrison, 1998: 8).

When researchers have followed the advice that, at debriefing stage, participants can 'complete their understanding' of the research (BSA, 1996: 2), they have sometimes found that this is restricted by the inaccessibility of the analysis to non-social scientists or participants less educated than themselves. Willis (1977), reporting on this aspect of his field research with school boys whose rejection of education he had analysed, found that the 'lads' could not understand his theoretical interpretation, but enjoyed reading the bits about themselves. That this is often so should not be surprising. Social-science knowledge is a highly specialised domain in which it takes time and extensive training to participate. The implication of this is that the understanding of research by participants would be an inappropriate principle on which to base ethical practice. Moreover, in our analysis, if our interpretations of our participants were psychologically close to the mark, we could expect their defences to work against them accepting our version of their worlds. In other words, in research based on our theoretical framework, we would expect disagreements over interpretation. Our own view is that, where there are conflicts of interest between researchers and participants, expressed in the form of disagreements over interpretations, publication or whatever, the researchers' responsibility should be to satisfy themselves that objections, alternative interpretations and other views of the participants have been taken into account, if only implicitly, in the writing up of the research. Beyond that, the ethical touchstone should be to ensure that the level of harm that might be predicted is no greater than that to which they have anyway been exposed.

Data in the public realm: a 'date-rape' case

Let us see how these ethical dilemmas associated with researching defended, psychosocial subjects work out in analysing a particular set of publicly available data. The research in question was prompted by a British 'date rape' court case involving two students, which received extensive newspaper coverage, but left us very unsatisfied with the sense made of it by the press. Specifically, we felt the 'either/or'-ism of the legal discourse of coercion or consent, guilt or innocence, failed to answer the questions implicitly raised in many of the press accounts of the trial. We therefore deconstructed these press accounts, and offered our own reading of events based on our premise of the defended, psychosocial nature of subjectivity. Our reading combined discursive and psychodynamic elements in emphasising the complex and contradictory nature of gendered identities involved in heterosexual relating. Our analytical goal was similar to that of our research into the fear of crime where we spoke to people direct. Our relation to the material in this case, however, was bound to be different as we were relating to people only through mediated press reports. However, the lack of a face-to-face relationship did not exclude the operation of unconscious intersubjective dynamics: in analysing these data we were undoubtedly influenced by our emotional responses and, as in all cases, they could work both as a resource (through identification) and as an obstacle (through the mobilisation of our defences).

We are not interested here in relating the substantive findings of that research (which can be found in Hollway and Jefferson, 1998). Rather, what concerns us are, once again, the ethical dilemmas this research presented to us, the inadequacies of existing ethical guidelines and our attempts to resolve these issues. As will become clear, the issues are neither clear cut nor easily resolvable. But, by concretely relating the ethical principles involved to research practice, we hope to make it easier to think them through.

Informed consent

When dealing with newspaper accounts, the issue of consent is rendered problematic in several ways. The central question is whether consent is necessary for words spoken by participants in court or in interviews with the press, that is, in a public context or one where words spoken would become public. We did try to secure the consent of the two principal figures since some of the early readers of our then unpublished work thought this might be a good idea on ethical grounds. The result was that one failed to answer and the other did so only through an intermediary, a college tutor, who raised a series of points and objections, and a request that we should not publish. Three further general points were raised during our deliberations about whether to publish, which we discuss below.

Is consent always necessary?

Our 'date-rape' case does seem to highlight the problems with the basic ethical principle of consent. Biographers who write about their subjects without permission are not seen as ethically inferior to the authorised biographers. If anything, they are less liable to the accusation of hagiography. Journalists who had to seek permission to write about anyone would simply not be doing their job. If Bernstein and Woodward had had to secure Nixon's consent before publishing the results of their 'research' into Watergate, whither the public exposé then? If it is okay for biographers and journalists to proceed without consent on the basis that their informants may have things to hide and that part of their craft (and duty) is to uncover the hidden or the secret, then why is it unethical if social scientists do so?

If the tutor's request that we should not publish can be read as a withholding of consent by our research participant, were we wrong to publish? In terms of the power relations between researcher and researched, the tutor who replied to us on behalf of the student was someone like ourselves in formal power terms. Our response to that intervention was respectful: we carefully read what he had to say and made certain alterations to our text where these seemed to be warranted. We replied to him with our judgements and information about our intentions. The differences between us were not to do with structural imbalances of power since there were none. Differences arose from our different interpretations of the case. Arguably, since he was the tutor of one of the participants, and very supportive to the defendant throughout the affair, his interpretation was less disinterested than ours.

Is there a limit to the issue of consent?

There are occasions when consent is not the primary ethical principle, but is contradicted by another. In the Watergate example above, this principle is the public interest. There are many other occasions when one ethical principle is contradicted by another. In certain areas of social-science research – areas involving illicit activities of various kinds, for example – informed consent is neither possible nor desirable. To get the research done at all, deception, in the form of covert research may sometimes be necessary (we shall have more to say on this below). In our particular example, a contested rape case, it is hard to imagine both parties, with their different stories, consenting to have their accounts 'refereed' (as it must seem to them) by a 'disinterested' third party: there is too much at stake. They need advocates to advance their interests, not researchers to question them. In this context, then, asking for consent is likely to be a pointless exercise.

The ability to say 'no' can be a powerful one in the research process and can be enough to counteract the otherwise powerful institutional and educational resources of the researcher. In our particular case, for the reasons given above, our retrospective attempt to secure consent to our project foundered on the silence of one party and the objections of the other's representative. Should we have allowed the implicit 'no' of one key participant to jeopardise the project when we considered the objections to be insufficient to warrant what would have amounted to self-censorship? We were wanting to voice ideas that were not getting an airing in the debate on 'date-rape' and which in our view were needed. Wherein should the power of veto lie, especially in contentious areas of public debate in which, by definition, disagreement is endemic? To give participants the power of veto over the re-analysis of the public accounts of their motives and actions would seem to be giving up on a founding idea of democracy, namely, free speech. Surely this cannot be what the guidelines intend?

Is there a need for the consent of all parties?

Another way of looking at the limit to consent in a case like this is to ask where it stops. We requested the consent of the two principals, but what of the bit players: parents, friends and other bystanders who appear in the story? Were they to be asked, should they have a right of veto by refusing their consent? In the furore caused by the publication of Gitta Sereny's second book, *Cries Unheard* (1998) on Mary Bell, the woman who killed two boys as a 10-year-old, the issue of consent was exactly this. The book is based on several months of taped talks with Mary Bell (then in her late thirties), who was painstakingly informed of the possible consequences of publication, but who none the less consented to the painful interviews and the disruptive aftermath (including her 14-year-old daughter finding out that her mother, as a child, had murdered two children). But both Sereny and Bell knew that Bell's mother (who comes across in an appalling light: neglectful, rejecting, sadistic and abusive of the young Mary) would never have consented had she been alive to ask. (The mother warned Mary repeatedly against reading Sereny's first book on the case, *The Case of Mary Bell* (1995), which was, according to the mother, 'full of lies' about her.) Nor would the parents of the dead boys be likely to have consented had they been asked. For them the book was a reminder of their loss; as Sereny commented, 'I know that their deep wish must have been never to have to relive the memory of those dreadful days, indeed never to hear the name of Mary Bell again' (Sereny, 1998: 384). Sereny wondered daily 'whether writing this book was the right thing to do' (Sereny, 1998: xix). Rather than ask the parents for their consent (which she knew would be refused), she justified her choice to publish for the sake of Mary's child: 'So the child … is, I think, essentially its *raison d'être* and even its justification' (1998: xix), though her long-standing interest in questions of 'evil' suggest that her motives were more complex than that.

Confidentiality

Rendering case material anonymous is, as we know, a fundamental guiding ethical principle. In biographical work like that of Sereny's, or the work one of us has been doing on the boxer Mike Tyson (Jefferson, 1996a, b, 1997, 1998), the uniqueness or recognisability of the material means that anonymity simply cannot work or would defeat the purpose of the research. In our 'date-rape' case we did not name the man in an effort to protect his identity (especially since he was acquitted). The woman was unnamed throughout, as is usual in rape cases unless she chooses otherwise. However, given the unique details pertaining to the case (despite the fact that we were interested in focusing it through its more general, socially significant features), we could not guarantee that the principal figures, or some of their friends or relatives, or anyone else for that matter, would not be able to recognise the case (which was headline news in the UK at the time) were they to pick up the journal in which we eventually published.

The larger question revolves around the fact that the material upon which we based our analysis of the 'date-rape' case was (and is) all a matter of public record and, therefore, by definition, not confidential to start with. In this case, it is not the material itself which is the focus of ethical consideration, but what researchers do with it; in our case, the use of it for psychosocial interpretation. We were utilising psychoanalytical terms, such as splitting and projection, to make sense of aspects of the behaviour of the participants but we were doing so on material which was not subject to clinical conventions of confidentiality.[8] For some, the interpretation of unconscious motivations should be confined to clinical settings where professional supports are available. Other standards may be more applicable in the public setting, however: not the clinical standard of confidentiality, but the educational one of informing the public. If so, the overriding issue becomes that of an honest and compassionate attempt to advance public understanding of a contentious political issue, through a critical engagement with the current debate, and advancing a particular argument supported by appropriate evidence.

There were some who thought we could circumvent the issue of confidentiality in two specific ways. First, we could focus our analysis not on the people concerned but their representation in the media. In other words, we would have to confine our analysis to media accounts of persons, without presuming to be able to 'read through' media accounts to the people being represented. By confining us to the level of discourse, this solution would have disabled our desire to reinstate a missing psychodynamic dimension to researching subjectivity. Secondly, we could produce composite, and hence fictional, characters through utilising details taken from several, similar 'date-rape' cases. This would have made a nonsense of our attempt to demonstrate how it is possible to make sense of unique details from a case only through a reinstatement of a psychodynamic dimension. Composites would have enabled us to 'cheat': to choose only the bits that made our case and disregard those that didn't. One could no longer use the criterion that adequate theory must be able to explain any given real-life case. Our method is more rigorous than that. Both suggestions ignore the centrality to our analysis of the psychosocial subject. Both suggestions also encourage a certain deceit, which brings us to the next section.

Deception

As we saw above, some would regard the 'deception' of focusing on media accounts, or of fictionalising the account, as ethically preferable to the risk of participants recognising themselves and the harm to them that might result. This suggests that deception is not always to be avoided on ethical grounds. But the larger issue raised by deception is this: according to our conception of the defended subject, self-deception is part of the human condition. We all deceive ourselves over some things since to do otherwise is often too painful; hence the need for our defences. In matters to do with our sexual relationship or our gendered identity we know from experience how vulnerable we can be: how much we need to protect ourselves. When subjects deceive themselves, they also deceive others if those others take at face value what they say or do. Hence the need for a new research strategy to delve behind appearances, and for a new ethics to match.

Of course, self-deception is not confined to research participants; researchers too can deceive themselves. This can happen by not attending to transference/countertransference issues in the research relationship; in other words, by mistaking our own concerns for those of the participants we analyse (see Chapter 3). Although we were not in face-to-face contact with the participants in our 'date-rape' research, these dynamics can still operate. A second form of self-deception can occur as a result of not having sufficient background information about family or other biographical details, and thus producing too speculative or 'wild' analyses. If the answer, for some, is not to try, our answer is to take the analysis only as far as evidence permits. We aim to acknowledge puzzlement where evidence is lacking, and admit we are creating, not 'truths' about a person, but an account which is methodologically, empirically and theoretically convincing. This issue of the 'truth', or otherwise, of interpretations leads us on to the vexed issue of 'harm' to participants. Defences protect us from potentially distressing 'truths' about ourselves. A 'truthful' analysis may not be able to avoid distress to the participant, but it does not automatically follow that distress is harmful, as we argued earlier in Fran's case.

Avoidance of harm

Some people's response to traumatic or distressing events is to leave well alone, since to re-enter them is to relive pain, difficulty, discomfort, hurt. Psychoanalysis challenges the belief that it is best to avoid distress. In contrast, it is based on theoretical principles which stress that well-being depends on making the causes of distress conscious, in a containing environment, where they can be discovered not to be threatening to the survival of the self. According to this model, it is not necessarily harmful if research raises painful and distressing experience, though it may be discomforting. The only route to the truth may be through causing the participants renewed distress. Gitta Sereny has spent much of her writing life researching distressing subjects: the commandant of the Treblinka death camp, Franz Stangl; the infamous Nazi, Albert Speer; and, as we saw, Mary Bell. This is Sereny's account of the pain she enabled Mary to go through in her attempt to get at the truth of how Mary came to murder her first victim, a 'truth' that Mary had never uttered before:[9]

> It is extremely difficult to describe the extent of her [Mary's] distress during the ten to twelve days in the early part of our talks when she spoke about the abuse she suffered, and then about the killing of the two little boys. For the first week of it, when she was staying with us in London, I was sure almost every evening that she could not possibly go on with it the next morning. During the second week, when she lived at home, and my husband and I stayed nearby, I doubted every day that she would turn up, because I didn't think she could put herself through any more of it. Although I knew that much of what she said was fantasy and evasion, I had still carefully limited my expressions of doubt, and formulated my questions as unaggressively as I could. However, about five months later, as we were nearing the end of our talks, facing her with the reality of it had become inevitable. I told her that I thought that there had been some truth in everything she had said to me about the killing of Martin, but that the evidence produced at the trial showed that most of what she said could not have happened. You cannot bear to remember it as it really was, I told her. But you must try. You must make another, final effort, to tell it honestly. In the final analysis, I told her, only the truth would serve the purpose of this book: which was, on the one hand, to tell the story as completely as it could be told, but also to use what had happened to her, and the reactions of others, as an example and a warning. 'I don't know how to do it', she said, 'I don't know if I can.' (Sereny, 1998: 347–8)

Mary did keep coming back to force herself to remember what consciously she had been strenuously forgetting all her adult life. To that extent she consented on a continuous basis, though she could not have known the extent of the distress she was letting herself in for when she agreed initially to talk to Sereny, as we discussed above in the more innocuous case of Fran. But that does not exhaust the issue of harm, about which Sereny got two conflicting views from the two psychiatrists she consulted. The first one 'was concerned over the unrelenting intensity of [the] … sessions which would normally, under therapeutic treatment conditions, have probably stretched over a period of years' (1998: 348). The second thought the sessions should continue ' "because she [Mary] urgently needs to say it" ' (1998: 348). In other words, the issue of whether the distress to which Mary was subjected was harmful or therapeutic was not resolvable. Beyond that there is the issue of the distress caused to Mary by the book's publication, the 'scandal' of her being paid for it, having to move, and having to tell her daughter that she had killed two children. Did Mary consent to all that? Was the distress all worth it? Will it continue to be worth it in the years ahead?

If distress is the midwife to truth when researching anxiety-provoking subjects, and if distress and harm are conflated, the 'no harm to participants' principle effectively precludes any interpretative work which assigns motives other than those admitted to by the parties themselves, since the impact of such revelations can never be wholly predicted. That position would make much published work 'unethical', including virtually all psychoanalytic, family therapeutic and psychological case histories. The idea of a critical social science could hardly survive such an ethical strait-jacket. Harm must be evaluated independently of distress.

Given this, the ethical issue for us cannot reduce to whether publication of our work on 'date-rape' might cause one or both of the two students distress were they to come across it. We assume the reminder would be distressing, but much else in their daily lives would also serve as reminders. It is possible that coming across our analysis could be helpful, not harmful. For example, if either or both of the students felt that their personal failings had contributed to the trauma of the events (and it is hard to believe that they would not fear that this was the case), it might be both illuminating and reassuring to understand their dilemmas in terms of the contemporary difficulties of negotiating gender identities in heterosexual relating. In the course of using our analysis with undergraduate students for teaching purposes, the excitement and relief of recognition has been notable.

The experience of recognition has a bearing, then, on our understanding of the risk of harm in the course of this kind of research. Recognition is not about reassurance, if that is based on the avoidance of distress and therefore unreliable in telling the truth. It depends on the feeling that the other can be relied upon to be independent, to reflect back a reality which is not compromised by dependence or avoidance.[10] To strive after this as the basis for an ethical relationship in research is to pursue the values of honesty, sympathy and respect.

Appropriate principles for researching psychosocial subjects

Honesty

For us, honesty entailed approaching the data openly and even-handedly, in a spirit of enquiry not advocacy, deploying a theoretical framework which was laid out and justified, making only such judgements as could be supported by the evidence, and not ignoring evidence when it suited us. It also involved interrogating our responses to the data. Our joint involvement enabled us to interrogate suspected lapses of judgement in the other (see Chapter 4 for an example). We might have wanted more biographical information than was to hand, and it would have helped to have been able to test our interpretations in some form of exchange with the students themselves in the 'date-rape' case, but all research suffers from limits to the available data. Within those limits, the issue had to be that of the integrity of the analysis, and whether, for all the shortcomings, there was some advance in the quality of understanding an experience. In this case, we believe that our analysis of the case was more experientially recognisable than that offered by the newspaper accounts.

Sympathy

Gitta Sereny approaches her subjects with sympathy: 'the fact or capacity of entering into or sharing the feelings of another or others; fellow-feeling' (*Shorter Oxford English Dictionary*). Her willingness to enter into the feelings of someone whose actions would appear to have put her beyond humanity in the case of Mary Bell shows a deep and courageous commitment to understanding a fellow human being. The view of Dr Raj Persaud, a consultant psychiatrist, by contrast, was profoundly unsympathetic: 'Mary Bell's outpourings appear to be a common rationalization that disturbed criminals make to try to justify their actions' (quoted in the *Daily Mail*, 30 April 1998: 7). Here, understanding of a person very different from himself has been replaced with the judgemental consignment of Bell to the ranks of a stereotypical 'other': 'disturbed criminals'.

Our treatment of the students in the 'date-rape' case, approaches them sympathetically. It accuses neither of them of evil or disreputable motives, nor treats them as blameworthy, alien or other. Rather, in analysing their confusions over their motives, stemming from their 'struggling with developing feminine and masculine identities on the difficult and dangerous terrain of contemporary heterosexual relating'

(Hollway and Jefferson, 1998: 406), we put ourselves alongside them, attempting to use what self-knowledge we possessed and the difficulties we were familiar with, to assist us to understand their 'inconsistencies, confusions and anxieties' (1998: 406).

Respect

While it would be inappropriate to treat everyone with respect in the sense of 'to treat or regard with deference, esteem, or honour' (*Shorter Oxford English Dictionary*), everyone is entitled to respect in the sense of 'to pay attention to; to observe carefully' (ibid.); and it is in that sense that we approached the subjects of our research. Part of our dissatisfaction with the one-dimensional newspaper accounts of the 'date-rape' case was that they were disrespectful in this sense: they were inattentive, careless observers. We attribute no malice here; the pressures and constraints of news production routinely promote disrespect of this kind. Researchers, on the other hand, have a duty to respect in this sense – it is perhaps their primary ethical responsibility.

Our view of our analysis of the 'date-rape' case, the participants, their relationship, the events before and during the night in question, is that we have been respectful. We brought to bear all the forms of knowledge – theoretical, empirical, experiential – at our disposal, and sieved the available data through these various knowledges, attending particularly to those bits of data that got stuck in one or other of our knowledge meshes, refusing the easy option of ignoring recalcitrant data. Although we could not secure the consent of participants, nor guarantee anonymity, nor ensure that publication would not cause further distress, we have proceeded with respect, even if, in so doing, we have noticed things that the participants would prefer to remain unnoticed. To respect in the sense of observing carefully is to notice what normally is overlooked, what might be too painful to notice. This 'warts and all' notion of respect is why it is possible both to 'respect the person' and to 'condemn (some of) their actions'. Sereny is respectful of Bell in this sense, Persaud is not.

None the less, our remarks may be read as disrespectful, just as, above, we argued that our interpretations could be experienced as harmful. Where, then, to draw the ethical line? Are researchers to be condemned for not predicting all the readings their texts might occasion? Is the plea of respectful intent naïve and therefore morally useless? If research participants may feel their intentions have been lost in the researchers' interpretations, might not researchers too have grounds for complaint when their intentions get lost in their readers' interpretations? Like Sereny, we have worried about these questions during and after the course of our research. The psychoanalytic concept of recognition is useful in this respect also. Benjamin (1995) argues that recognition is as important to psychological survival as food is to physical survival. In order to achieve a differentiated self, every person needs recognition from another who is independent of his or her own omnipotent wishes, which include desires to be seen in an unequivocally good light. In this sense we need 'true recognition' – a realistic appraisal independent of our own self-serving defences, even though this may be uncomfortable. Of course, this depends on the other being honest in the sense of not being driven by his or her own defensive needs. If recognition is communicated in a spirit of sympathy and respect, it is more likely to be acknowledged rather than rejected. The concept of recognition can thus point towards the ethical principles of honesty and respect.

Summary

- The ethical guidelines currently on offer were tested in terms of their ability to assist three of our research cases.

- In each case, our presupposition of a defended, psychosocial subject rendered the ethical guidelines' key notions of informed consent, confidentiality, deception and avoidance of harm at best problematic and, at worst, misguided.

- We mapped out the contours of a more adequate approach: one in which the ethical principles of honesty, sympathy and respect would be central.

Notes

1   As the British Sociological Association (BSA) notes, 'Because sociologists study the relatively powerless as well as those more powerful than themselves, research relationships are frequently characterised by disparities of power and status' (1996: 1).

2   Consent is central to ethical guidelines. For example, 'Psychologists shall normally carry out investigations or interventions only with the valid consent of participants, having taken all reasonable steps to ensure that they have adequately understood the nature of the investigation and its anticipated consequences' (British Psychological Society, 1996: 2). Likewise, the BSA stipulates 'as far as possible, sociological research should be based on the freely given informed consent of those studied. This implies a responsibility on the sociologist to explain as fully as possible, and in terms meaningful to participants, what the research is about, who is undertaking and financing it' (British Sociological Association, 1996: 1).

3   For example, the British Psychological Society (BPS) recommends that 'an experiment in which negative mood was induced requires the induction of a happy mood state before the participant leaves the experimental setting' (1996: 5). This unidirectional model of a researcher inducing an effect in someone is a far cry from the situations we were dealing with.

4   Hinshelwood (1997) makes the same point when he talks about the impossibility of informed consent to psychoanalytic therapy.

5   These issues are found in the preliminary statements of ethical guidelines (for example, 'Good psychological research is possible only if there is mutual respect and confidence between investigators and participants'; BPS, 1996: 7), but an understanding of their expression in the research encounter is usually abandoned in favour of a set of technical guidelines which emphasize set behaviours as opposed to the moral principles underlying those behaviours.

6   In their consent definitions, both the BPS and the BSA acknowledge that there can often be a conflict of interest between the purposes of research and the principle of getting informed consent. Psychology, because of its history of using deception in its experimental research, has been particularly conscious recently of the conflicts of interest in ensuring informed consent. Psychology has a vexed history concerning deception and ethics. The scientific method was seen to depend on the naïvety of subjects, as in Milgram's study of obedience (1974) when subjects in a laboratory experiment were deceived into thinking they were administering electric shocks.

7   See Hinshelwood (1997: Ch. 9) for a detailed consideration of the implications of the Kleinian concept of splitting for the principle of informed consent.

8   However, psychoanalytic or psychotherapeutic case studies are increasingly finding their way into generally available publications. Scharff includes a dedication to his patients which raises many of the same issues of anonymity and disguise. He hopes that they can 'tolerate the revelation of my experience not revealed to them during treatment, given here in the interests of a scholarly and educational endeavour' (1992: xvii). Woodward (1996) discusses the experience of finding her case written up in a journal in the course of her researches.

9   It took Mary many years to admit, even to herself, that she had killed the child, and several sanitised versions over the years, before she could manage this.

10   For a theorisation of the importance of intersubjective recognition in coming to terms with painful aspects of identity, see Benjamin (1995: Ch. 1).

CHAPTER 6

BIOGRAPHY, DEMOGRAPHY AND GENERALISABILITY

Thus far, we have explored the theoretical, methodological and ethical implications for the production and analysis of data when working with a psychosocial subject; that is, one theorised as constituted from a combination of unique biographical events (in which unconscious dynamics are crucial in determining a person's relation to external reality), and socially shared meanings, interactions and situations. The question we need to address in this chapter concerns the generalisability of knowledge produced by these methods. Our answer entails several stages. Specifically, this chapter is our attempt to:

- clarify why generalisability is a contentious issue in the debate about the reliability of knowledge, especially in relation to case studies;
- show how we dealt with the tension between demographic and biographical data in designing and analysing our research into the fear of crime;
- demonstrate the problem of using demographic similarities among research subjects as a basis for generalised explanations of the fear of crime;
- illustrate the heterogeneity of meanings obscured by 'same-coding' profiles;
- use one of the clusters produced by our analysis to explore the issue of the generalisability of our findings;
- draw out the lessons for the production of research knowledge on the fear of crime.

Generalisability, knowledge and case studies

Abbott (1992: 62) makes the point that 'we generally think that only individual cases can really "be narrative" [that is, tell stories] and that only population studies can really "be analytic" [that is, do science]'. This conventional confusion stems from a false dichotomy, as Edelson (1988) also argued. All science, whether based on a case study of one person or a whole population of persons, is interested in 'abstracting out aspects of reality – properties of interest (ultimately variables) – in order to investigate just the relations between or among these'

(Edelson, 1988: 89). Moreover, all studies involve the testing of rival hypotheses against the available evidence: 'the same kind of reasoning about hypothesis and evidence may be used', whether the 'domain' being studied is 'a single person, single cultural object or a single society, organisation, group or family' (1988: 91).

In our particular cases, our wide-ranging enquiries into the complex realities of people's lives were not pursued for their own sakes; rather, this route was undertaken in order to understand, as comprehensively as possible, the relations among the aspects of reality (or variables) of ultimate interest to us, namely the fear of crime, risk (of criminal victimisation) and anxiety. Similarly, the uniqueness of our subjects' biographies were not primarily of interest in themselves; rather, their importance was consequent upon the theoretical importance we attached to a biographically derived concept of unconscious anxiety. Our analytical procedure of testing our hypotheses against rival hypotheses in the light of all the available evidence also conforms to the mode of scientific reasoning described by Edelson (1988).

So, single-case-based studies and population-based studies are not incommensurable 'even if it is not ... possible to provide evidence from a study of [one] case that would justify generalising the same hypothesis to other cases' (Edelson, 1988: 92). If so, how could we establish the generalisability of any of our findings drawn from a single case study and the limitations of such generalisations? This was the challenge as we attempted to apply our theoretical arguments to overview the evidence from a whole series of cases; namely, for us, 37 of them, selected originally to reflect the differences in the fear of crime found in the British Crime Survey; that is, sex, age and high- or low-crime residential location.

The tension between demography and biography

The existing debate on the fear of crime, as we saw in Chapter 1, is premised almost entirely on demographically based comparative generalisations: between women's and men's fear of crime, older and younger people's and those living in higher- or lower-risk locations. Since we wished to contribute to this debate, our research design could hardly ignore such demographic factors. Given our theoretical interest in how anxiety affected the fear of crime, we also needed biographical data to enable us to track over time the meanings for individuals of fear, risk and anxiety. These tensions manifested themselves at all stages of the research: tensions between our wish to illustrate and explain how a person's unique history of anxiety affected their fear of crime, on the one hand, and, on the other, to be able to comment on the existing literature's concern with sex and age differences and disagreement over whether fear was predicted by risk of criminal victimisation. In this section we set out how such tensions affected our research design and whole sample analysis.

In designing our sample, we took three factors, or variables – location, sex and age – which, according to survey research, affected fear of crime. We aimed to interview equal numbers in each of these categories. The resulting sample is represented in Table 6.1. The number in each group was dictated by both pragmatic and theoretical considerations: our commitment to an in-depth method meant that 37 double interviews, each lasting between 60 and 90 minutes, would produce as much data as we could properly analyse, given the time-frame. But is three in each group enough? Enough for what? (The question is a product of the dominance of statistical methods which need large numbers for tests of statistical significance.) Could we make generalisations and comparisons based on such a sample? The tension between depth and breadth evidenced here is a common one which echoes the polarisation of qualitative and quantitative research.

This is where the purposes of the research have to be clear. We wanted to mount a challenge to the realist proposition that people's fear is simply related to their risk of victimisation (and therefore to their high- or low-crime location). This meant, according to our theoretical approach, investigating fear, risk and anxiety in two such locations. For the purposes of our theoretical challenge, we needed to be able to demonstrate the existence of people whose fear was not simply related to their risk, and we needed to explain their fear in a more plausible way. If we could explain the people whose fear did seem to be in proportion to their risk within the same theoretical terms, that would be even better. We wanted to talk to women and men, old and young, in order to explore the implication in the literature that young men's lack of fear conformed most closely to this realist model and that those whose fear was greater than their risk were irrational (see Chapter 1). If we found sex and age differences, we did not just want to add these to the over-abundance of such findings, but wanted to explain them, both those which conformed to the research findings (in the case of fearful older women, say) and those which did not (in the case of fearful young men or fearless older women perhaps).

Table 6.1   Our interview sample selected to reflect variables of location, sex and age

Location	Young (17–29 years)		Middle-aged (30–54 years)		Older (55 + years)	
	Men	Women	Men	Women	Men	Women
High crime	3	3	3	4	4	2
Low crime	3	3	2	3	4	3

Thus our sample design was decided on the basis of a set of theoretically driven research questions (as well as practical considerations) and not on the basis of what numbers would be adequate to make a generalisable claim about the differences between groups. None the less, there was a comparative element to our design which required that we found a way to look at similarities and differences within groups (based on location, sex and age) as well as analysing individual case studies.

The significance of one element in a person's story was best understood when it was seen in the wider context of everything that we had been told by that person (see Chapter 3) and we were reluctant, therefore, to break up the whole into categories which could then be compared to others' accounts on the same theme. We found ourselves being pulled, almost irresistibly, towards the analysis of case studies. These, we believe, were faithful to the unique histories, circumstances and meanings of our interviewees. In Chapter 3, our account of data analysis reads as if we proceeded exclusively via in-depth, case-based analyses. Not so. For the reasons we have introduced above, we aimed to conduct a comparative analysis which was none the less faithful to our theoretical principles about the self, especially about meanings being revealed in the context of the whole and having unique, as well as shared, characteristics. We had to find a way of performing a comparative analysis of our data, without sacrificing the complexity and uniqueness of people's stories.

In summary, while our analysis would be based on our three key concepts – risk, fear of crime and anxiety – and we had also to remain faithful to our respondents' *Gestalts* in making sense of their stories, it was essential to devise a way of comparing information across categories.

Since our data were largely structured by each person's unique free associations, we had little structure common to the totality of the data with which to work. However, we had used a structured set of questions with each interviewee, which meant that we had some equivalent data on each. We tried to use all the information at our disposal to ask if and how the relations among risk, fear of crime and anxiety varied, in our small sample, according to age, sex and high- and low-crime residential location.

We proceeded in three stages:

1 We evolved a set of *categories* through which to operationalise our questions.
2 We could then *code* each interviewee on each category (high, medium or low) so as to provide a schematic way of comparing individuals or groups across those categories.
3 We *clustered* interviewees according to identical codes on risk, fear of crime and anxiety.

Categories

Our categories were not derived prior to our fieldwork, as in most research, where the data analytical categories mirror the questions that were posed to respondents. They emerged from trying to make sense of the meanings of risk, fear of crime and anxiety in the interview transcripts of each individual. For example, what did risk of criminal victimisation mean, except in the light of people's resources, such as owning a car – especially for women? But then, having evolved a category for information on the resources which affected the risks people had in common, we found that, to use this consistently, we had to expand it in order to take into account the fact that some people's resources were more personal, for example, a belief in God. This might affect their risk adversely, but diminish their fear. For example, Dick was an evangelical minister who, as a result, was taunted and harassed by some locals. However, his religious belief acted as a cloak against fear. The meaning of 'risk' to our respondents revealed further complexity. For example, when we asked 'Can you tell me how risk has impacted on your life since you have been living here?', we got different answers, some emphasising risk-taking exploits, others being at risk. Furthermore, given our theoretical presupposition that people's own motivations and behaviour are not always transparent or truthfully known, we did not always take interviewees' own assessment of their risk-taking at face value.

In summary, the categories were part of our analysis, not prior to it: they emerged out of a grounded theory approach where theory and data informed each other at every stage. However, the more we subdivided categories to be sensitive to differences, the more these risked fragmentation, thus threatening the whole that gave them their meaning. Should we go down the route of increasing fragmentation or try to hold together each of our three key concepts? We did try the first route before settling on the second. In some instances fragmentation was useful. For example, we devised eight categories to subdivide people's experiences of criminal victimization,[1] as well as another four for risk.[2] By turning these into tabular form, we were able to establish to our satisfaction in what sense the high-crime estate did increase risks of victimisation and for what categories of resident. However, this is straying on to well-established terrain and away from our purpose here.

Coding

For the purpose of making comparisons, we needed a way of coding people on each of our key concepts. First therefore we devised an 'at risk' coding for each interviewee, on a 'high', 'medium', 'low' scale, taking into account history of criminal victimisation, lifestyle (precautions taken, risks run etc.) and resources. The idea of reducing the complexity of individual accounts of risk to a three-point scale (high, medium, low) is a radical step and inevitably oversimplifies. This step is mitigated by the fact that we kept each whole case in view. Our use of a scale represented the translation of our judgements, based on several categories, into a single value on a scale which could then be used for comparison. However, the same value did not necessarily mean the same thing.

For example, we coded two of the young men (Sam and Winston) at medium risk, despite their caution, because they were liable to be picked upon. All the young women on the high-crime estate are medium or high risk, but for different reasons: Cherie because she hangs out with some rough youths on the estate; Rachel because she is the daughter of Dick (the evangelical 'Jovo'); and Jane because she is an 'outsider' and a single mother with two mixed-race children living on the worst road on the estate who has to leave the house unoccupied some evenings. The others at high risk were Dick (the 'Jovo') and Liz, a police informer who spent a lot of time in the rough, local pub. The low-risk stories exhibit similarly unique combinations of age, location, lifestyle, resources and precautions, a point we illustrate below through the cases of Phil and Juliet. The use of a three-point scale is shown up in these examples to be an analytical device, defined both theoretically and in terms of our familiarity with all of our case data, which enabled potentially interesting comparisons about risk.

The route to our codings for fear of crime and anxiety was similarly protracted (we will leave out the specific detail we have illustrated in the case of risk). Again, our interviewing produced a range of narratives, reflections, details of practices and speculations relevant to the fear of crime stemming from initial questions about safety and fear, follow-up questions, as well as the specific questions which came at the end. At this stage, then, we had three codings for each interviewee, representing our judgement – based on all the information that we had mustered into a *Gestalt* – of their levels of risk, fear and anxiety on a three-point scale, high, medium and low (see Table 6.2). We called this a profile. Our profiles had the advantage of showing us the relations among the three factors at a glance. We came to realise that these relations were more important conceptually than each coding on its own.

Coding is a questionable step to take with qualitative data based on principles of preserving meaning within biography and social context. It reflects, surely, the dominance of a quantitative tradition which has little compunction about reducing complexity to single scores. However, this tradition has the advantage of being able to handle large data sets. So, despite our misgivings, we set out to see if the profiles helped us to see patterns and groupings within our 37 cases.

Table 6.2   **Risk, fear of crime and anxiety profiles**

		1 Risk	2 Fear of crime	3 Anxiety
Young	Mark	H	L	L
men	Craig	H	L	H
HC	Ron	H	L	H
Young	Sam	M	M	L
men	Billy	L	M	H
LC	Winston	M	M	H
Middle-aged	Harry	M	L	L
men	Tommy	L	L	H
HC	Dick	H	L	L
Middle-aged	Duncan	L	M	H
men	Phil	L	L	M
LC				
Older men	Martin	L	M	M
HC	Roger	L	M	H
	Hassan	L	H	M
	Jack	L	L	L
Older men	John	L	M	H
LC	Arthur	L	M	M
	Graham	L	L	M
	Len	L	L	M
Young	Cherie	M	L	H
women	Jane	H	M	L
HC	Rachel	M	L	L
Young	Linda	L	H	H
women	Juliet	L	L	M
LC	Ann	L	H	H
Middle-aged	June	L	H	H
women	Kelly	L	H	H
HC	Liz	H	M	M
	Joyce	M	L	M
Middle-aged	Fran	L	H	H
women	Jackie	L	M	M
LC	Dawn	L	M	M
Older women	Maureen	M	M	H
HC	Ivy	L	L	H
Older	Dot	L	L	H
women	Barbara	L	L	L
LC	Brenda	L	L	L

HC, high-crime estate; LC, low-crime estate. H, M and L indicate high, medium and low on a three-point scale.

Clustering

Grouping profiles which matched on all three dimensions (risk, fear of crime, anxiety) reduced 37 individual profiles to 16 clusters (see

Box 6.1). Six of these contain only one person, and so are inappropriate to consider as clusters, and in a further four the numbers are too small (two per cluster) to constitute a meaningful cluster (though they may be indicative). In the remaining six clusters, demographic characteristics show up in some of these, but they never totally defined the cluster. For example, even the most coherent cluster, number 14 (low risk, high fear of crime and high anxiety), which consists of five women (and to which we return below), straddles the young/middle-aged and high-/low-crime location categories. Cluster 4, which consists of four men, straddles all the age categories and both high- and low-crime locations.[3]

Box 6.1   Sixteen clusters based on shared risk, fear of crime and anxiety profiles (H, high; M, medium; L, low)

1   *HLL: Highly at risk, not fearful, but relatively unanxious*
    Two men: Mark and Dick, both from the high-crime estate, neither of them old.
2   *HLH: Highly at risk, not fearful and highly anxious*
    Two young men: Craig and Ron, both from the high-crime estate.
3   *MML: Somewhat at risk and somewhat fearful, but relatively unanxious*
    One young man: Sam, from the low-crime estate.
4   *LMH: Hardly at risk, somewhat fearful and highly anxious*
    Four men: Billy, Duncan, Roger and John, all except Roger from the low-crime estate.
5   *MMH: Somewhat at risk and somewhat fearful, and highly anxious*
    Two people: Winston and Maureen, with only the profile in common.
6   *MLL: Somewhat at risk, but neither fearful nor anxious*
    Two people: Harry and Rachel, neither of them old, both from the high-crime estate.
7   *LLH: Hardly at risk, not fearful, but highly anxious*
    Three people: Tommy, Ivy and Dot; the first two, son and mother. None of them was young.
8   *LLM: Hardly at risk, not fearful, and somewhat anxious*
    Four people: Phil, Graham, Len and Juliet. All were from the low-crime estate and three were not young.
9   *LMM: Hardly at risk, but somewhat fearful and somewhat anxious*
    Four people: Martin, Arthur, Jackie and Dawn. Nobody was young in this group and three came from the low-crime estate.
10   *LHM: Hardly at risk, but highly fearful and somewhat anxious*
    One old man: Hassan, from the high-crime estate.
11   *LLL: Hardly at risk, not fearful and relatively unanxious*
    Three people: Jack, Barbara and Brenda, all of them old.
12   *MLH: Somewhat at risk, not fearful, but highly anxious*
    One young women: Cherie, from the high-crime estate.

13   *HML: Highly at risk, somewhat fearful, but relatively unanxious*
     One young women: Jane, from the high-crime estate.
14   *LHH: Hardly at risk, but highly fearful and highly anxious*
     Five women: Linda, Ann, June, Kelly and Fran, two from the
     high-crime estate. None of them was old.
15   *HMM: Highly at risk, somewhat fearful and somewhat anxious*
     One middle-aged woman: Liz, from the high-crime estate.
16   *MLM: Somewhat at risk, not fearful, but somewhat anxious*
     One middle-aged woman: Joyce, from the high-crime estate.

The way that age, sex and location are so frequently mixed within the clusters shows that the effects of demographic factors are cut across by other factors. The four ethnic minority interviewees (John, Winston, Martin and Hassan) were also spread across the clusters. However, when we look across the ten clusters with more than one person in them, there is some weak demographic patterning, and sometimes in the expected directions (for example, clusters 2 and 14).

If we look at two of our key variables, age and sex, across the clusters, to what extent do these reflect the variable of high- or low-crime location and how much effect do they show in people's risk, fear of crime and anxiety profiles? Age is significant in more of these clusters than our other variables, sex and location. For example, in seven out of ten clusters (clusters 1, 2, 6, 7, 9, 11 and 14) either the young or the old are absent. Often, this age patterning appears to derive from a common low-risk factor in the two older-age groups (clusters 7, 9, 11 and 14) in contrast with the high or medium risk of, in particular, the young men (clusters 1 and 2). Risk interacts with location, which, however, seems to have a weaker influence than age: clusters 1 and 2 show high risk and high-crime estate; clusters 8 and 9, low risk and mostly low-crime estate.

What we see in these patterns is a reflection of the lifestyles adopted by most of the middle-aged and old people, irrespective of estate, which meant routinised, highly local lives which were largely home-based. The lifestyles of some, but not all, of the young women were more likely to follow this pattern than the young men's. These lifestyles, though, were not necessarily motivated by fear of crime.

What of different patterning between the sexes? Four of the ten clusters consist of only one sex (clusters 1, 2, 4 and 14). It is apparent that sex is affecting the relation between the young and risk, clusters 1 and 2 being all men. Higher-risk women, where they cluster at all, are separate (clusters 5 and 6). Why, then, might there be fewer systematic differences in risk between women of different ages? To answer this, it is important to go back to the earlier stage of our analysis and remember that the risks on which our scores are based are different for men and women: many of the women did not go out unescorted after dark because this was experienced as constituting a risk specifically of male sexual violence. Their risks were judged to be low for this reason, irrespective of the fact that official crime figures revealed no incidents of public sexual violence on these estates. The higher fear of crime than risk, characteristic of cluster 14, is largely accounted for by the pattern common to young and middle-aged women of fear of male sexual violence (to which we return below).

Such clusters with their weak demographic patterning are a rather meagre basis on which to construct other than the most tentative generalisations about the contribution of demographic categories to the fear of crime. The reason for this, as we have been arguing throughout, is the need to consider biographical as well as demographic factors. Trying to explain fear of crime profiles on the basis of demographic factors alone is doomed to failure, as the examples in the following section forcefully remind us.

The problem of using demographic similarities

In this section we compare the cases of two women, Kelly and Joyce, from among 37 people whom we interviewed in the course of our research into the fear of crime. You have already met both these women: Joyce in Chapter 2; and Kelly in Chapter 4; Kelly was the third member of the Walters family we interviewed, along with Tommy, her older brother, and Ivy, her mother. We selected these two participants because they were strikingly similar in terms of demographic characteristics. They were aged 34 and 36 respectively, were brought up on neighbouring streets on the high-crime estate where they both lived. Each came from a large family, one of nine and eight siblings respectively. Each was absent from the estate when first married (for eight and ten years respectively), moved back subsequently and bought their house from the council. Each has family close by. Each has four children and is separated from the father(s) of their children, though Kelly is remarried. Each has a part-time, unskilled, typically gendered job.

Given these demographic similarities between Kelly and Joyce, how did two such similar women express such differences in their fear of crime: Kelly, highly fearful despite her low-risk situation (one of the low risk/high fear of crime/high anxiety women in cluster 14); Joyce, relatively unafraid despite her somewhat riskier situation (a medium risk/low fear of crime/medium anxiety profile which placed her on her own in cluster 16)? Realist theory would predict that Joyce's lower level of fear would be the result of a lower level of risk and less history of criminal victimisation. Actually, Kelly's risks were lower than Joyce's because she lived with her husband, a large dog and ever-present watchful neighbours on the respectable end of the estate. Their histories of criminal victimisation on the estate were very similar, both quite minor. Our search for the meanings of risk, fear and crime for Kelly and Joyce led to the discovery of their remarkably different relationships to the estate on which they both lived. In other words, although their social location – past and present – and direct experience of crime on the estate were almost identical, their biographically based psychological locatedness was strikingly different. We believe this to be an expression of the different role that anxiety played in their lives.

Kelly: a pen portrait

Kelly is a woman who has lived nearly all her life on a high-crime estate, but whose most direct experience of victimisation on the estate is the theft of her husband's van.[4] This immediately serves to problematise any simple relationship between her risk and her high fear; the more so since this experience of victimisation occurred when she was ensconced in the respectable area of the estate, where she feels safer from the risk of criminal victimisation. This distinction between different parts of the estate is central to Kelly's fearful concern with crime. Although she takes a range of precautions, these become extreme when she goes to her brother's house, less than half a mile away on the rough part of the estate; the area she calls 'little Belfast'. There she 'pips' rather than get out of the car, even in broad daylight.

Kelly was born on the high-crime council estate where we conducted our interviews. She was the youngest of a family of nine, though since the family took in her sister's illegitimate child, she had, in effect, a younger 'brother' (actually a nephew) whom she was obliged to look after, something she profoundly resented. At 12, her father died, after which 'there were no one there to love me.' At 18, she got married 'to get away' and only returned to the estate eight years later. During her time away, she had one child with her husband, but then left him for a man with whom she was 'besotted', who became increasingly violent over the course of three pregnancies (one a miscarriage resulting from his violence). After being hospitalised and deciding to press charges, which subsequently put her partner in prison, she returned to the same road where she had grown up, close to her mother and a brother. She was 'a complete wreck', dangerously underweight, with three children. She felt ashamed and anxious: 'I used to think everybody were looking at me and talking about me ... that's more paranoid than ... being unsafe.'

Over the course of the next two years, her feelings about the estate were transformed from being her family 'territory', which she 'really loved', to a place where 'I don't fit in their territory' because of the 'nightmare' of crime. During this time she met the man whom she subsequently married. Their now mutual dislike of the estate was catered for when they moved into, and subsequently bought, a house half a mile away in what is widely regarded as the respectable part of the estate. She speaks of her present location as 'off the estate', though it is geographically central. Her contrast between the two locations is between 'paradise' and 'little Belfast', despite the fact that she was never a victim of crime prior to her move, but only since.

Kelly: anxiety, respectability and fear of crime

As we saw in Chapter 4, Kelly's concern with respectability dates back to her adolescent fear of sexuality and getting pregnant.[5] We saw how this was linked to her mother Ivy's lifelong preoccupation with sexual respectability. This concern (which did not disappear, as it rationally might have done, after her white wedding supposedly secured her own and her mother's respectability), combined with Kelly's fearful investment in discourses of local crime, provides the most salient clue to her determination to describe herself as living 'off' the estate. We picked up this clue by paying attention to our initial confusion (it was one of the first things she said when we knocked on her door) rather than pursuing logic and consistency. By asking what emotional or identity purposes this served, by immersing ourselves in her position via her stories, and by deploying a theoretical framework emphasising the centrality of defences against anxiety, we could make sense of what might have been rejected as nonsense. We could then make links to her biography more generally.

The effect of positioning herself as 'off' the estate is to situate crime somewhere else (albeit only half a mile away), in 'little Belfast', thus preserving her crime-free 'paradise'. The polarisation of meaning in these two terms suggests a paranoid-schizoid splitting of bad (little Belfast) and good (paradise). This serves the purpose of locating the good – safety, security and respectability for her self and her family – where she now lives. As predicted within Kleinian theory, there is a cost to her relation with reality, namely her refusal to acknowledge that her current location is also 'on' the estate. Many others alluded to the distinction between rough and respectable parts of the estate, but only Kelly used the 'little Belfast'/'paradise' metaphor, and referred to her part as being 'off' the estate altogether.

However, Kelly moved between this paranoid-schizoid position and a more reality-based one, for example, when she said 'I'm sure, from estate, it'll eventually work its way down.' Thus she not only takes extreme precautions 'there', as we saw when visiting her brother, she also worries about crime where she lives, pointing anxiously to a neighbouring house where a 'problem family' might be moving in, leaving her house open to risk. Yet, she does not believe she is at risk of burglary, given her large dog and ever-alert neighbours. Instead, we can posit that her concern with 'problem families' is less to do with the risk of burglary by delinquent children, and more to do with the threat to her recently achieved respectability ('I've been a problem family'). In this light her fear of crime has more to do with the respectable distance it puts between her and those she was brought up with who have not moved (including her brother) than a likely place to put her anxieties for her own and her family's safety.

An endorsement of this reading may be found in her understanding of anxiety. When asked about times when she'd felt anxious, she answered 'what, to get away? … I were anxious to move off estate … very, very, anxious.' (This is an example of the importance of not imposing one's own meaning on the interviewee. Her association here gave us a further valuable clue to her identity and desires.) Now she is 'off' (in her terms): 'I'm anxious to get on. I'm wanting more and more and more.' What this insatiable desire for a rosy future suggests is a wish to escape from her past: from a big, rough family; from her mother's projected shame; from the unrespectability of bearing two, mixed-race, illegitimate children to an abusive man. All this fear of the past is lodged with the estate (though it does not all rightfully belong there): 'If I'd have stayed on estate, I'd 'ave been in a worse state … and probably still a one-parent family.'

Though she has managed to move only half a mile from her past (and even less from her mother), she needs to have made it 'off the estate' – out of the rough, into 'paradise'. This motivated, unrealistic reading of her present situation is assisted by her present husband's strong identification with respectability for them both: '[he] used to like – I suppose brain wash me into like – saying "It's a right estate … what's a nice girl like you doing on estate?"' Once we took note of Kelly's shame about her past we could make good sense of her particular form of investment in the fear of crime, her strong commitment to respectability, especially to being 'a proper family', and her idiosyncratic relationship to locality.

Joyce: a pen portrait

Since a pen portrait and brief analysis of Joyce were given in Chapter 2, we shall present her case more briefly. Aged 36, she was born on an adjoining road to Kelly, one of eight siblings. Now, after ten years off the estate, starting when she got married (similar to Kelly's eight-year absence), she lives with her four children in her original family home (on the rough end of the estate, in the centre of what Kelly calls 'little Belfast'), which, like Kelly, she has bought from the council. A sister lives close by.

Unlike Kelly, Joyce is often on her own in the house since she has no husband and her children spend time with their father, but she does not seem fearful. This does not mean she feels invulnerable; rather, her knowledge of the families on the estate is used to give her a general sense of safety, quite the opposite of how Kelly used the same local knowledge. Such knowledge sometimes needs to be actively cultivated to produce a feeling of familiarity, and hence security. She illustrates this when she says, of the first times when she was left on her own, 'I weren't frightened ... everybody used to go 'ome at night from pub ... it could be quite a game for me, 'cos I could tell you who voice were.' Coming from the rough end of the estate did not compromise her sense of respectability. Unlike Kelly, her own and her children's respectability does not depend on putting a distance between herself and the estate.

Joyce: anxiety, local identity and fear of crime

Joyce believes that being a known local protects her from crime because of the principle that you do not steal from those like yourself. However, she realises that the protection afforded by such a principle is under threat from young local drug addicts, as evidenced by the theft from her garden shed. Yet, because she went to school with some of the local criminals, and some helped her out when her husband left, she does not see them as threatening; on the contrary, they are local 'softies'.

These beliefs work to protect Joyce from constructing a dangerous 'criminal other'. They enable a balanced view of the reality of local crime, an ability to hold on to the 'good' and the 'bad', and indicate that the depressive position is accessible to Joyce in this arena. This is not to say that she is always capable of such balanced views. To the extent that Joyce does not wish to know about drugs, has an irrational fear of black people (despite the reality of her 'smashing' black neighbour) and holds to a notion of 'lone parent families' spoiling the estate (albeit qualified by her recognition of her own similar status and the real issue being about how you bring your children up) we saw this as evidence of 'splitting' behaviour: of Joyce moving from a depressive to a paranoid-schizoid one. However, such evidence of splitting was far less evident in her relationship to crime than was the case with Kelly.

The fact that Joyce's risk/fear calculations are relatively realistic is, then, a result of her identification as a local. Joyce, in contrast to Kelly, is determined to hold on to the possibility of being local *and* being respectable, despite the tension posed by rising crime and drug-use on the estate and her fears for its effects on her children. As a result, she has a tendency to downplay (but not to deny) local crime and to emphasise her local identity, which is based on a happy childhood and, until her husband left, a trouble-free life. Identifying closely with her mother, she is committed to stemming the downward slide of a locality which represents the most cherished aspects of her self, including her dead parents. To this end, she takes risks by challenging and reporting young criminals, something which many do not do, for fear of reprisals. When threatened by one boy in this way, her robust response, reportedly, was: 'You piece of shit …You think you bother me? … I've lived round 'ere years. Take more than you to frighten me luv.' Her respectability does not stop her talking rough. She thereby ensures that she is not cast as 'them', rather than 'us', by local criminal youths. Her stability and relative freedom from anxiety partly account for her low fear of crime, but this stability is tied in to a local identity which has the effect of mediating her relation to local crime in a direction which emphasises the unthreatening, familiar identities of local criminals who have principles.

Demographic similarities, biographical differences

In summary, the similarity between Kelly and Joyce's demographic profiles is incapable of accounting for the crucial differences which lead to their contrasting relations to the fear of crime – differences which are at least partly explained by the paranoid-schizoid or depressive forms that anxiety habitually takes, according to Kleinian theory. Expressions of their anxiety come out in the different meanings of localness and their different relations to it as part of their identities: Kelly rejects the estate in search of respectability, while Joyce embraces it in the hope of preserving the security of a local identity. Their respective fear of crime is a part of these wider differences in meanings concerning their relation to the high-crime estate, meanings which reflect neither the demographic similarity of their past and present location, nor their experiences of criminal victimisation.

If the effect of biography is to render incommensurable women like Kelly and Joyce who in demographic terms are all but identical, the same is also true of two people with identical risk/fear of crime/anxiety profiles. In other words, it is a mistake to assume, as a realist might, that identical profiles can provide an easy basis for generalisation because they must have been achieved via similar biographies. The next section illustrates this point in a concrete fashion.

The heterogeneity of meanings obscured by 'same-coding' profiles

In this section we look at an example of how even people with the same risk/fear of crime/anxiety profiles, which might appear to suggest some similarities in their lives or lifestyles, can turn out to be very different. In other words, while sensitive clustering of the sort attempted in this chapter can assist the search for comparative generalisations, it can never replace the importance of the individual case. Our chosen cases, Phil and Juliet, are taken from cluster 8. They display low risk, low fear of crime and medium anxiety. Within a realist theory of the fear of crime, neither would require any explanation.

Phil and Juliet: same profiles, different meanings

Phil is a 53-year-old man, too poor to own a car, who has lived, crime-free, with his wife, adult stepson and two teenage sons on a low-crime estate for the past six years. His time is mostly spent locally on activities related to his role as Neighbourhood Watch coordinator, in committee work or visiting the elderly. An only child, Phil claims that his childhood and schooldays were happy. Thereafter, disappointments dogged him. Forbidden from joining the RAF by his father (which left him 'deflated'), he worked 12-hour shifts in the local bakery. After his mother died, he cared for his ailing father, which prevented him from taking up a new career in teaching. His father's death quickly followed, and he was made redundant, a two-year period he described as 'difficult'. Getting married in his mid-thirties seemed to help at this point but, three years into a new job in a new city, a freak and apparently minor accident to his elbow at home 'shattered' his life. It forced him to retire at the age of 39, and left him 'semi-disabled' – arthritic, and unable to do simple household tasks – and feeling 'a burden'. He is also blind in one eye.

Phil's characteristic way of coping with these 'slings and arrows' has been to throw himself into activities on behalf of others. This community-mindedness stems partly from his early upbringing in a mining village where it had been instilled in him to 'always think of other people's safety as well as your own' (his years as an active trade union representative attest to this legacy). And it stems partly from the need to do something now he can no longer work: to fend off boredom and stop himself 'going daft'. But there is also evidence that his self-imposed round of community activities is part of a defensive structure in which 'other people's needs' are constantly seen as 'more greater than mine'. Asked about earlier anxieties in his life, he replied: 'No, only for other people.' Asked about his own safety, he replied: 'Well, I always try to give other people safety.' Such extreme other-centredness in response to questions about himself is highly significant in the light of his own situation as a multiply-disabled, jobless man in poor health.

Phil's messianic concern with community safety provides evidence that displacement is characteristic of his defensive structure. It is true that he picked up a strong sense of the importance of being safety-minded from his father who, having fallen off some scaffolding as a young man and having had his abdomen 'ripped out', became very safety conscious as a building contractor responsible for others in similar situations. His thwarting of Phil's RAF ambitions were to do with the risks attached to flying. Later, Phil's trade-union years were dominated by health and safety concerns. At one time he was regional vice-chair for health and safety and later, knowing he was finished with work, he went on a union-sponsored health and safety course. So, in many respects, it is unsurprising that when Phil had to give up paid work, and instead took up voluntary work in the community, issues of community safety should become a core focus. But that fails to explain the somewhat obsessional way in which Phil has approached his community role: for example, his determination to set up a Neighbourhood Watch scheme on a high-crime estate where he lived previously, despite apathy ('nobody wanted to know') and outright opposition from those who didn't want a 'police-estate'. This included a vendetta against him and his family by one local teenager which involved five arson attempts over nine months. It led to them being rehoused in their present low-crime location. Though he describes this whole time as 'a frightening experience', his first associations, characteristically, were to the welfare of others in the block of maisonettes if the fire had caught. Also characteristically, he transformed a frightening personal experience into something that 'made us more aware on 'ealth and safety grounds of other people as well as meself'.

The threat to his family appeared to affect neither his fear of crime ('I don't worry about crime for myself') nor his keenness to be involved in Neighbourhood Watch activities. Once settled on his new estate, he continued to campaign for the establishment of a Neighbourhood Watch scheme, this time successfully. But not content with matters of crime, such as issuing the elderly with personal alarms and talking to the council about improving the area's lighting, he sees danger everywhere. For example, wet leaves in Autumn constitute a threat to the elderly, and so he is campaigning to get the council to cut down the beautiful, old broad-leaved trees which line the estate's roads.

Considering Phil's low risk, low fear of crime, moderate anxiety[6] scores in the light of the above, we can see how misleading were first impressions. When seen as ways of coping with anxiety, his disclaimers about not being fearful of crime 'for himself' make a new sense in relation to his extreme responses to community dangers and his excessive concern for the safety of others. His long-standing fears about safety, bequeathed by his father and reactivated throughout the traumas of his own biography, were projected on to the safety of the elderly.

Juliet is 25 years old and has lived for 20 of those years in the same house on the low-crime estate where she still lives. Her present risk and fear are both low, largely because she rarely goes anywhere without her boyfriend, with whom she has lived for five years, and whom she trusts deeply.[7] The house has never been burgled.

Juliet's biography would lead us to expect considerable anxiety, which, however, might not manifest itself in fear of crime. Her mother resented her from birth, for reasons which Juliet only worked out in her teens. Then she discovered that her father had disappeared on the day that her mother gave birth to her – a cause, she considered, for the resentment and lack of love that her mother showed her. When her younger sister was born, her jealousy led Juliet to attack the sister constantly. This led to the regular, harsh physical punishment that her mother dealt out to her. The risks she was wont to take when in her teens resulted from this experience: 'I used to think I were indestructible when I were younger ... I'd 'ad it all – you couldn't 'urt me.' Her claim clearly puts this feeling in the past; since this time her relationship with her mother has improved enormously. She also claims that she has 'always' felt an intense fear of rape, which, like many women, has some basis in particular, distressing experiences. For example, Juliet talked of having been 'extremely upset' when some lads from her school year, while messing around with a group of girls in the park, playing a game of forfeits, got her top off and later tried to pull off her trousers. She bit one lad so hard that, according to her, he must still have the scar, though she added that she never believed that they would rape her. According to her, rape is her worst fear – and this remains the case, feeding into, and probably feeding off, her boyfriend's strong feelings of protectiveness towards her. The terror that rape holds as a threat to her core self was conveyed by her claim that she would 'flip' if it happened; that is, she would lose her sanity. This is one place where her anxiety feeds into her fear of crime. It may account for her rather fearful tendency to avoid pub doorways when walking home from work on winter evenings.

The other suggestion of 'excessive' feelings accompanying her experience of criminal victimisation was over her car. This had been stolen twice, and had also had items stolen from it. When she went with the police to reclaim it, she said she had felt 'horrible' about the car, so much so that she ceased to enjoy it and sold it soon after. Her strong feelings were conveyed in the interview long after the event. These implied that her identification with the car was so great that she herself felt violated by its theft and the wanton damage that had been done to it. Her first car had been given to her by the grandparents whose reliability and care had provided the only respite from her own family. Her subsequent relationship to owning a car appeared to contain many of the positive feelings associated with this relationship; the external threat of the car being stolen signified an internal threat of considerable proportions. As a result, she would have felt intensely at risk if she had still owned a car, a threat she preferred not to experience.

There was also evidence that Juliet's money worries, which she reported as her main worries, were a site for the safe expression and control of her biographical anxieties. She and her boyfriend were indeed faced by the threat of debt, since both of them were in low-paid jobs. Whereas his response to this reality had been to avoid it by spending what he had, for example on a huge collection of CDs, Juliet's approach was to control their joint income tightly. The result was that they rarely went out, every bill was anticipated and they never got into debt.

In summary, we believe that Juliet's low risk/low fear conjunction is not adequately explained as a realistic calculation of the risks she faces. While the main reason for her low risk and low fear is contingent on the internal and external security she has experienced as a result of her relationship, there is some evidence that anxiety feeds into aspects of fear to do with sexual safety, which for her is profoundly connected with the safety of her core sense of self. While her relationship helps to mitigate her anxiety and to contain her fierce anger at her position in life, her approach to money serves to channel anxiety into an area where she exercises some real control.

The similarity between Phil and Juliet's profiles does not imply that risk and fear of crime mean the same thing in each case. Once anxiety is factored in, their similar profiles, albeit achieved by unique biographies, become explicable, as we have tried to show here. We could have chosen other examples to make the same point. However, we trust that the general point about the need to be sensitive to the individual case behind identical profiles has now been established because, in the next section, we wish to discuss the most coherent of our clusters (14) in terms of what we might be able to generalise from it.

The generalisability of our findings

Cluster 14 consists of five women (Linda, Ann, June, Kelly and Fran) who are similar with regard to their fear (which we judged to be excessive) of being out on their own after dark. This theme, remember, has been central to the realist position about the relation between risk and fear of crime. The five women do not all live on the same estate: June and Kelly live on the high-crime estate; the others on the low-crime estate. All of them have a child or children, except for Linda, aged 17, who lives with her mother and brother. June's husband is unemployed and is usually at home, while Ann's husband has a job which takes him away a lot. Linda depends a great deal on her boyfriend and Fran recently moved on to the council estate (from a private one) when she separated from her husband after more than 15 years. Their worries about crime centre on known dangers: notably burglary and physical and sexual assault. Each has relatively low records of victimisation, but Ann's appears to have been more threatening.

Characteristic of each woman was a fear of being out by herself after dark (or even in daytime except locally). Linda has always feared walking alone after dark. In this connection, she remembered hearing, when she was about eight, that a rapist lived round the corner. Now, after college in winter, she arranges for her boyfriend or mother to meet her. She doesn't like being in the house alone and follows her mother's example of asking callers for identification before she lets them in. Recently, Linda's fears seemed justified when a man, posing as a gas company employee, tried to gain entry to her home. She remains fearful even though she coped with the threat and he did not get in. Ann remembers being warned of the danger of being out after dark by her parents and was afraid by the time she was 11. June says she is very wary around people; even a tap on the shoulder in broad daylight by someone she knew would cause her to jump. Kelly, as we saw earlier, is afraid to get out of her car even in broad daylight when visiting her brother on the street next to the one she grew up on (she may have been more afraid for the car than for herself). She expected her husband to put the car in the garage at night, but if he was away, would only do so accompanied by her large dog. Fran's recent fear of crime centres on her fear of male sexual violence, illustrated by her experience, at a bus-stop outside the hospital in the middle of the day, of a somewhat shady-looking man who was the only other person there. She waited for the bus imagining how easy it would be for this man to overpower her, pull her behind the wall and rape her. Inside the home her fear is similar: after being out with her mother and step-father, she obliged her step-father to check the house for hidden intruders before he and her mother went home.

This is a common feature of women's lives and arguably reflects a realistic assessment of the risk to women of sexual assault, which may be improbable, but would be extremely serious. None less it did not characterise all the women we interviewed. Rather it seemed to be a defining feature of a fearful femininity in which anxiety had become attached, often from an early age, to the idea of being the victim of a male stranger when unprotected. Fran's daughter (but not her son) is learning her fear: she is fearful walking the short distance home from her friend's house on winter evenings, even though it is along a busy well-lit road.

The other side of this coin is the experience of security that women habitually feel when they are accompanied by a husband, male partner or male family member. As in Ann's case, who only sleeps soundly when her husband is back, we heard time and again from women that they felt safe both inside and out as long as their man was with them. The capacity to protect appears to be projected on to known men, despite the practical protection that these women are involved in as mothers, wives and daughters (where it is called care). The ensuing lack of a sense of control is likely to be experienced as vulnerability to criminal victimisation, notably by strange men.

Fran, aged 35, has recently split up with her husband and moved on to the low-crime estate from a private housing estate with her two teenage children. This life change has precipitated fearfulness in instances where risk remains the same. For example, only since then has she been afraid of flying. Fran's anxiety seems to cover for an intense – and perhaps temporary – anxiety about being a single woman, lone mother and council tenant; that is, a loss of many aspects of self on which she had depended. Her fears are not simply a response to the new external threats associated with being a single, unescorted woman since she led a social life very separate from her husband while she was married and was not fearful. She closes the front curtains at dusk because, as she explained, she doesn't want people to know her business. This account, which on the surface was about fears of burglary and intrusion, pointed to a deeper fear that she would be seen by others as a lone mother, belonging to a category of women who are doubly stigmatised, for supposedly failing as mothers and as women by not having a man. There is a further piece of evidence that her fears of sexual assault are displaced: when her daughter telephones to be escorted back home after dark from a nearby friend's house, Fran's worries are all for her daughter and not for herself, evidenced by the fact that, at these times, she walks out to meet her daughter without worrying about her own safety.

Both Linda and Fran have memories of violent and alcoholic fathers assaulting their mothers (who both subsequently left their marriages and brought their children up single-handedly for many years). It may be that their excessive fears of strange men are a repository for anxieties about men precipitated early in their lives, but kept separated from their feelings about known men: neither have any reason to fear known men now. (Kelly and June, on the other hand, were closer to their fathers than their mothers.)

In short, the higher anxiety and fear of crime, not commensurate with risk, illustrated in this group of women reflects a specifically gendered expression of anxiety. This involves an unrealistic projection of control and the capacity to protect into known men. It manifests in a gendered fear of crime, where threats to the self and the extension of these into their children (especially daughters) are experienced as coming from other men – strangers who are imagined to be threatening.

Let us now look at the way in which we can understand this phenomenon more generally, using a combination of *Gestalt* and the clustering method which we are illustrating. In the results of survey research, the preponderance of women who may fear sexual assault is camouflaged in the blunt gender difference in the fear of crime. When it has been the subject of other research, women have been asked directly about their fears of sexual assault and this has confirmed its importance in women's lives. It has been seen as a realistic response to a real (and serious) danger. The differences among women are rarely made visible nor, when they are, explained.

In these cases, we see girls' early and formless anxiety being channelled into a fear of strange men, specifically through a widespread worry about girls' safety on their own after dark. There are real and serious risks to boys, too, of predatory paedophiles, but rarely do boys introject such fear and it normally does not become a receptacle for their anxiety (as in Fran's children's case). For women, fear of strange men continues to be available as a receptacle for anxieties when these are precipitated by events, as in Fran's case in her recent change of circumstances. The biography of such women is in this respect a biography of the recursive channelling of anxiety into a culturally sanctioned, gender-specific fear (of strange men's sexual predations). This explanation does not exclude the effects of real events, such as Linda's narrow escape from what could well have been sexual assault. However, biography is not a direct reflection of real events. Rather, past experiences are continuously reconstructed in the light of later meanings (Scott, 1996).

While the above explanation emphasises the role of unique biographies, what we are explaining also has a social dimension in the sense that these fears are expressed almost exclusively by girls and women. However, because of biographical features, not all women are positioned by this discourse of female sexual vulnerability. We have explained these biographical features in terms of anxiety: it may be that people are subject to very different levels of anxiety, as a result, for example, of how secure their early experiences were. It is also the case, so we are arguing, that people cope with and defend against their anxieties by using different channels, of which fear of male sexual assault is just one. In summary, in looking at these women's biographies, even at this superficial level, we can see the way in which demographic and biographical features are jointly expressed in their fears of going out on their own.

A test of this psychosocial argument would be if it could explain both differences within a demographic group, such as differences between women, and similarities which bridge different demographic groups, such as men showing a similar profile to women. Rachel, a 19-year-old woman living with her family of origin on the high-crime estate, is an example of a woman who, unlike those just discussed, is not particularly fearful when she goes out at night. Her profile (medium risk, low fear, low anxiety) is higher on risk than most of the women for two reasons: first, because she has been harassed locally for being a 'Jovo' (religious), on account of her father, and secondly, because she travels late on public transport and walks through the estate (she does not have a car, though her boyfriend does). She returns after dark from her job and regularly travels alone to and from a gym, which involves two bus journeys, changing at a city bus station which gets quite rough with groups of drunken youths at night. Although this does not feel safe, she has never been assaulted. On the basis of experience, therefore, she continues her solo leisure activities after work. Our explanation here would go into Rachel's biography to test two possibilities: either that her anxiety is channelled elsewhere or that she is 'depressive' in her capacity to face anxiety-provoking situations without sacrificing her grip on reality. Although we have not the space to go into detail here (but see Joyce's case), we found plenty of evidence for the latter interpretation.

We can use Hassan's case (on his own in cluster 10) to illustrate how similarities can bridge different demographic characteristics. His profile (low risk, high fear, medium anxiety) is similar to the above group of women, though he is marginally less anxious, but he differs from them on most of the demographic categories that were designed into our research (namely, sex and age) and also 'race'. Hassan, an older man (aged 68), who now lives alone, is highly fearful. An immigrant to England in his late teens, he remained single until his forties. He then had a marriage arranged with a much younger woman who joined him in England and they had five children in quick succession. These were happy years; everything was 'smashing'. He was fulfilled as husband, father and provider – and unafraid. Then his wife began to challenge his authority, eventually leaving, taking the children. Later he was persuaded to sign over his half of the house to them, leaving him nothing. Then his health gave out, he retired early from his job as a nursing assistant and now spends his days in considerable pain.

Now – which seems to refer generally to his years as a divorced, retired man living on the estate – everything is 'terrible'. He is frightened to go out after dark, rarely doing so except to pray during Ramadan, when he usually gets a lift. At home he is afraid to open the door and jumps when the fridge makes a noise. Watching the TV is scary, with stories of old people getting killed. He talked repetitively of all this 'pinching and killing' frightening him, and all the elderly, 'to death', yet had only ever experienced racially abusive behaviour (on two occasions, both mild) and ill-behaved kids knocking on his door and throwing a stone at the window.

Judged by either his present experience of life in a fairly protected corner of the estate in purpose-built accommodation for the elderly, or his 'smashing' past experience as a happy family man and worker, his present fears are, we suggest, excessive and invested. Clues to the purpose served by Hassan's defensive investment are to be found both in his account of his marriage breaking up and the fact that his vehement tirade against crime is part of a general tirade against the ills of modernity, including sexual permissiveness and drugs. A traditional, conservative, religious man, Hassan's marriage broke down when his wife challenged his patriarchal right to order her life. A younger woman, she chose modern independence over traditional religious and patriarchal authority – as did their children in going with her. The loss of all he ever worked for has left him lonely and disappointed, with a painful old age ahead. His devout and fatalistic Muslim beliefs serve to contain some of his anxiety. However, the fact that he appeared to channel his feelings of loss into fear of crime suggests the need for a bearable fear to replace his deep loss and how threatening it would be to acknowledge.

Hassan shares a set of practices with his age group in terms of going out very little. Like many older men (see Roger in Chapter 2), his fear of crime is inflected with comparisons between the past and present, although in his case this carries a religious and cultural significance too. As with Roger, these comparisons achieve their significance biographically. Hassan's vulnerability to racist harassment and assault provides an external parallel to women's vulnerability to sexual attack, but there is not the same insertion of this vulnerability into biography as with the cluster of women above. Hassan was free of such fears as a young single man and a family man. There is an echo of Fran's recent fear in the way in which his fear of crime follows the losses to his self-identity, though his were more severe. This is a reminder that psychological mechanisms to do with coping with loss and trauma and ways of defending against anxiety cross demographic boundaries, as well as often being articulated in gendered – and other social – ways.

Lessons for the production of knowledge on the fear of crime

The key lesson we have learned from our efforts to work with biographical and demographic data is the irreducible character of the psychosocial, as we have demonstrated throughout. One person's unique defensive structures cannot be simply read off from their social, demographic characteristics. This may be a hard lesson for criminologists concerned with the fear of crime[8] to come to terms with, but a necessary one if we wish to move beyond the sterility of consigning fear 'surpluses' or 'deficits' to the catch-all, and incomprehensible, category of the 'irrational'. We are all more or less 'irrational' subjects. The point is to explain the relationship between the rational and the irrational in human behaviour; not to stop when we have reached the limits of the 'rational'.

The lessons for the limits to generalisability may be similarly hard but equally necessary: unless the individual case is kept in mind at each stage of the analysis, similar demographic characteristics or profiles will either produce spurious, misleading generalisations or so many exceptions to the rule that the (generalising) point of the exercise all but disappears under them. For certain purposes, the most general picture (with all its inaccuracies and exceptions) is what is required. Our purpose in the fear of crime project, if you recall, was stimulated precisely by the paradoxes such misleading generalisations had thrown up: the 'irrationally' fearful older women or the fearless younger men. In other words, the general picture of the fear of crime was so full of contradictions that it was becoming less and less useful for any purposes; worse still, it was becoming a self-fulfilling prophesy. This is not a plea to prioritise the individual case study over studies designed to produce generalisable findings, but it is a strong reminder that generalisations which have not taken account of biographical as well as demographic data are unlikely to prove a very useful basis upon which to advance either academic research or public policy debates.

In the next and final chapter we move from our whole sample analysis to a single case study of one of our interviewees in an attempt to produce a thorough exemplification and overview of our psychosocial approach.

Summary

- We argued that individual case studies are subject to the same scientific reasoning as population studies, though evidence gained from single cases cannot simply be generalised to other cases.
- The design for our research into the fear of crime reflected a tension between our desire to contribute to a debate in which demographically based generalisations dominate and our interest in how a person's biographical history of anxiety affects their fear of crime.
- We illustrated the analysis of our sample of 37 by categorising questions, coding interviewees and clustering those coded identically, and concluded that the demographic patterning revealed by clusters was a weak basis for generalisation because of the influence of biographical factors, illustrated by the cases of Kelly and Joyce.
- Even interviewees who had been coded identically turned out to be very different, once biographical factors and resultant personal meanings were taken into account, as the cases of Phil and Juliet revealed.
- An all-women cluster was explored in terms of the psychosocial (biographical and demographic) origins of their shared positioning within a discourse of women's sexual vulnerability. These women were then contrasted with a woman whose fear of crime was low and a man whose fear of crime was high, in order to test our analysis across clusters.
- It was concluded that generalisations about the fear of crime need to be based on biographical as well as demographic factors.

Notes

1   These were: burglary; other property and car crime; stranger violence; non-stranger crime; non-stranger violence; incivilities; violence in family of origin; criminal commission.

2   Our four risk categories were: precautions; risk-taking (self-report); risk taking (interviewer assessment); at risk.

3   We tried several other methods of clustering, including some based on looser matches, in order to try to ensure that more clusters were meaningfully sized, numerically speaking. These only compounded the problems we discuss here, hence our decision to use only this one 'same-profile' method of clustering in our discussions.

4   Our criterion that victimisation had to be estate-based eliminated her horrendous experience of partner violence from this particular reckoning, but we take account of its impact in our subsequent analysis. This criterion was necessary to preserve the status of our high- and low-crime location variable. Biographically, it makes little sense. This decision provides another illustration of the tension between the demographic and biographical approaches.

5   For an extended analysis of respectability and anxiety in Kelly and two other family members, see Hollway and Jefferson (1999).

6   The difficulty of putting a single score on Phil's anxiety demonstrates the dangers of simplification. Arguably Phil's anxiety is high but successfully coped with by its investment in community safety. The difficulty highlights the importance of theory: is anxiety low or high when it is successfully defended against?

7   See Hollway and Jefferson (unpublished) for a detailed analysis of the effect of her heterosexual relationship on her feelings of safety.

8   The point is equally applicable across the social sciences.

CHAPTER 7

A PSYCHOSOCIAL CASE STUDY

In this chapter we use a single case study to illustrate and overview a psychosocial analysis of subjectivity; that is, to demonstrate what we can produce using the method and theory described in the foregoing chapters.[1] This also entails discussing the relationship between researcher and researched in this case study.

We do not try to produce the story and explanation of a whole life as biographers tend to do. Ours is a more limited goal, yet one that depends on an understanding of Ron's *Gestalt*. We want to explain Ron's relationship to crime. In his case, this means his relationship to a series of criminal activities which have dominated his life since he was a child. We are interested in the ways that these are part of who he is. Although we interviewed Ron in the course of our research into the fear of crime, it was clear from Ron's answer to the first question that his relationship to crime was one of doing it rather than fearing it. We had anticipated this possibility, and our interview questions did not preclude eliciting this rather differently focused story. His reply to the initial interview question ('Can you tell me, Ron, about how crime has affected your life, or impacted on your life since you've been living here?') made just this point: 'Way, it's got me like most of what I've got.'

Researching Ron

Given our theoretical emphasis on unconscious intersubjectivity and how it affects the production and analysis of data, we will also look at our own relationships to Ron and to crime. Like Ron, we, the researchers, bring a biography and its attendant meanings to our relationship to crime. Our relationship to Ron's criminal acts will affect both the interview dynamics and how we make sense of his account. Tony interviewed Ron. Wendy, at the same time in the same house, was interviewing Ron's best friend, Craig, who shared many of his criminal exploits. We listened to Ron's first interview together to get two points of view prior to formulating the questions for the second interview. We wrote the psychosocial case study together, but drawing on these two different positions. This enabled us to triangulate. In this section, then, we ask (a) what is Tony's (and what is Wendy's) relation to crime; and (b) what is Tony's (and Wendy's) relation to Ron in the interview and as he comes through from the transcripts?

In order to write what follows, we discussed our relationship to Ron and his crimes. We focused on Tony, since he was the primary researcher in Ron's case. There are three facets of Tony's biography that illuminate his relation to crime:

- He is a criminologist; that is, he has a professional interest in crime, chose to specialise in it and can draw on substantial theoretical and empirical knowledge about it.
- As a young man he had direct experience of criminals and 'nutters' and a risk-taking, masculine, working-class English culture.
- He knows of criminal acts – albeit isolated – in his own family.

For these reasons, he is not distanced from crime but feels he can understand what it means from the inside and tends to feel sympathetic to those who commit (certain kinds of) crimes. None the less, he disapproves of burglary, seeing it as nastier than some other crimes because it can seriously frighten its victims.[2]

Tony is clear that he did not feel moral condemnation of Ron. This was especially so for two reasons: Ron's childhood experiences and how he comes over now as a decent person. Ron had evidently suffered a great deal of emotional neglect as a child, which he had survived quite well. He was not malicious and Tony felt that he had struggled (and continued to struggle) for moral integrity within the constraints of his life situation. Tony can contrast Ron with some criminals he has encountered who were hard, violent men, full of hate. He also felt he had known from his own youthful encounters the vulnerable side of hard-men and 'nutters'.

This meant, Tony felt, that he brought into the interview a sympathetic relation to Ron's account of crime that Ron would have felt safe in the telling of. Of course, Ron would have related to Tony through his own inner fantasies about this researcher. What did these feel like? For evidence, we have the tape and also Tony's feelings about how he was related to (the countertransference). From the tape it is clear that Ron became much more relaxed as the interview proceeded: he spoke more fluently and there were far fewer pauses. None the less, even at the beginning, when the account sounded very stilted, Ron was quite frank about his criminal involvement. It sounded as if he increasingly enjoyed talking to Tony. However, Tony felt that the relationship wasn't personalised as, for example, with Tommy. Ron was not relating to Tony as a differentiated person: he might have been any sympathetic professional – say, a probation officer – for all it seemed to matter. Probably the age difference between Tommy and Ron was significant. Whereas Tommy and Tony were of similar age, Tony was probably the age of Ron's father (indeed, Tony has a son of Ron's age).

As we have illustrated in the case of Tony and Tommy (Chapter 4), one way we can pick up on possible false notes in the analysis is through triangulation: did Wendy, from her different position, notice things differently? Wendy shares none of the influences which we reckoned were relevant in understanding Tony's relation to Ron as a criminal, yet she too warmed to Ron. Probably her feelings about Craig, Ron's best friend, are more telling because she interviewed him twice. Her differences from him on all the group identity categories which are routinely cited as being problematic for research interviewing could hardly have been greater (sex, class, employment, age, education – the only shared feature was being white). Craig not only had a prison record, but had been a heroin dealer (and addict). What made it possible to feel sympathy with Craig across these differences?

In both our cases, we reckoned it was something about Ron's and Craig's preparedness to face the reality of their actions. Neither denied that they caused people harm, nor blamed anybody but themselves. We do not know what they might be like in other contexts (both talked about sometimes feeling 'right paranoid' when they had had too much alcohol), but in the interview setting both came across as capable of maintaining a depressive position when viewing their lives. Both were, we thought, more decent now than they had been at their worst. Since we were both capable of identifying with (empathising with) their difficulties, we respected them, through the accounts they gave.

Could this not have been an artefact of a certain genre of storytelling? This was the interpretation put forward at a workshop we gave. In this view, Ron was constructing a narrative in the genre of reform or, in more old-fashioned terms, the triumph of good over evil. The purpose of such a narrative would be to elicit sympathy and approval for having struggled to reform oneself, a purpose which apparently had worked for Ron with Tony. Certainly Ron's account made many references to moral issues, both in relation to his criminal activities (for example, not stealing from children's bedrooms, which we analyse below) and beyond. Another example of a narrative genre interpretation was the idea that Ron was telling Tony 'horror stories' (about his life). Even if there is some truth in this, we do not regard it as a sufficient, or even central, explanation.

We are interested in how the 'reform' narrative was used with regard to how well it fitted with actual events in Ron's life: a 'reform' narrative does not fit *any* lived life. Our judgement that this narrative was fitting in Ron's case could be made through the detail of the stories and the indisputability of something very like what he was claiming to have happened. This is where we can rely, at least to some extent, on our method because of how close it stays to actual events. There are two sets of relations where the fit of narrative with reality is at stake. The first is: when Ron gives his account, how governed by reality is his remembering? The second is: how are we convinced (or not) by a person's telling and its truthfulness? We can only get at the first through the second. Of course, Tony's relation to the account affected Ron's narrative production too. Perhaps it was because he had sympathy for the theme of reform that it became as salient as it did (but it was only one of several salient themes). Again, this does not cast doubt on the veracity of the events, only acknowledges the truisms – that events are mediated in the telling (by discourses or narrative genres or forms) and also in the dynamics of the relationship within which the account occurs. To acknowledge these arguments does not necessitate giving up claims to be able to judge the truthfulness of accounts.

Ron: a pen portrait

When we interviewed Ron he was 24 years old, living with his girlfriend and their six-month-old daughter, in a council house on the same road where he has lived most of his life. The road is commonly recognised as the worst road on one of the worst estates in that city. (In Kelly's terms, it is in the heart of 'little Belfast'; Jane – see Chapter 3 – lives on the same road.) Ron's mum lives just round the corner, with her boyfriend, their two children, and Ron's younger sister. His mum also looks after Ron's daughter while his girlfriend works 'cutting lemons' for a business supplying pubs. Ron spends his time with other men from the estate, including his oldest friend, scouring the vicinity for anything that might be taken and sold for scrap; a form of thieving that he sees as less risky than burglary. Though Ron still does the occasional burglary, he regards himself as having given it up, partly because he does not want to risk imprisonment and the separation from his child that that would entail. Now he is more likely to be imprisoned for non-payment of fines; but since the time involved on such occasions is short, two weeks or so, he does not worry about the prospect.

Though Ron can remember living with his mum, dad and sister (and remembered his parents' rows), his salient early memories involve his mum going off to live with a younger man elsewhere on the estate, when he was around five or six. Then, he and his sister first stayed with their dad and then went to live with their grandmother for a couple of years, a move that also entailed a change of school, before moving back on to the estate to live with mum, her new boyfriend, mum's sister and her boyfriend, and changing school yet again. During this period, Ron had a bit of an 'attitude problem', as he put it: a problem that manifested itself in a combination of aggressiveness towards others, self-destructiveness and a reckless disregard for the consequences of his actions. He thought that he 'ran street' then. He was off his head, other kids were frightened of him, nothing mattered, and he could get away with anything. He mentioned head-butting walls, pulling all his hair out ('I once fucking plucked mesen bald'), splitting a kid's head open with a house brick (the kid having done something to his sister), and 'flipping': 'Every so often I'd just flip ... I'd 'old everything back, then just flip.' This was the reason he gave for taking some scissors to school in order to stab a kid who had done something to him. He also fought his sister, something that worried his mother enough to take him to see a psychologist. His mother thought he was copying his dad, who used to beat her up.

As well as his attitude problem, Ron also remembered from the same period nightmares about being poisoned. One time, he refused crisps from strangers – a promotional giveaway – when he was in town with his nan, fearing that they might be trying to poison him. He knew there was something wrong, since he would not normally have refused a free offering: 'owt for nowt', as he put it. Later he was afraid of taking tablets: 'at one bit ... I'd make mesen badly for days ... rather than take summat.' More generally, 'I've always been right wary about owt ... what goes into my body.' The exception, which he cannot explain, is glue-sniffing. Though he does smoke and drink, he never used to smoke, being 'frightened to death' even to pass an ashtray. As for drink, he's still 'funny' about how much he drinks, and only does it for the 'buzz'.

Moving back in with his mum did not help matters He did not get on with her boyfriend, who he thought sold off his toys, among other things. The man he looked up to, his live-in uncle, was a burglar (with his mum's boyfriend) and a local hard-man: he 'more or less fuckin' run estate: ... 'e 'ad a right lot of respect round 'ere ... 'e'd just walk round gennel, beat somebody up for owt ... just off 'is 'ead ... people were just generally frightened of 'im.'

Ron did what he wanted, which included roaming far into the surrounding countryside. This he did increasingly as he got older, wandering for miles with an older boy, being 'right adventurous' and 'right inquisitive'. Empty buildings or barns had to be explored 'even if there were nowt there'. Even with 'barrels saying toxic fuckin' poisonous and don't enter', they had to go in and have a look. Ron was also a collector of keys, which he would take along on these trips, but his curiosity was not confined to buildings. Anything, whatever it was, had to be examined: 'Like I climbed trees and that, and put me 'ands in 'oles and things like that.' This curiosity apparently motivated his first burglary. When they got into an old woodyard office, having 'gone through everything else', it dawned on him, for the first time, that what they were doing was more than a bit of fun. They found keys in a safe, 'they were the first to go', and £40 in a cash drawer. With his half of the money he 'bought all daft things, 'cos I'd never 'ad money like'. Part of the money went on clothes since he'd only had hand-me-downs. From this time on, 'I brought mesen up', as he put it. He was about ten or eleven.

On his first night-time burglary, he slipped out around 11 p.m. to meet his mate. They both dressed in black and wore balaclavas. It was still a game, but also real: they 'thought it were big time'. Their object was a council hut on the estate, which Ron thought held the keys to all the houses on the estate. The police were called by someone who saw them on the roof and they were caught. A first court appearance and a conditional discharge followed. It didn't bother him: 'nowt like that bothered me.' It seemed to bother his mother only to the extent that it bothered her boyfriend, but Ron had ceased to be frightened of his threats. After that, he was into everything from firms in the countryside to garden sheds, though not yet occupied houses. It was all part of messing about, daring each other and having a laugh. If there were things of value, they'd take them; at other times, like when they got into a steelworks and 'didn't know what were worth owt', they just had a laugh on the forklift trucks. On one occasion they did not rob a church collection box because the church had left the key on the gate, inviting visitors in and thus enabling them to shelter from the rain. Ron also said he would not burgle from the old, nor from children's rooms. Getting caught never appeared to be a threat.

Ron enjoyed his primary school experience and did well despite early difficulties associated with the series of changes of school. However, his move to secondary school did not go well. With all the new people, he could not find a place; and, despite being in the top groups when he was assessed, he 'felt better going out wagging it and … going out exploring'. After six months he became a regular truant. The burglaries became more serious with the transition to occupied houses. At first, these would be off the estate because you 'shouldn't pinch off people you know', though he admitted to having no qualms about thieving from those living nearby so long as they were on a different road. But, as Ron's liking for money and taste for drinking developed, the ethic of not pinching from your own kind broke down. Now Ron claims to have robbed every house on the estate.

During these early teen years, Ron felt 'untouchable' as a burglar: 'I could climb owt. I could run like shit … just right confident.' He wasn't bothered whether houses were occupied or not, and would even feel under the mattresses people were sleeping on. Sometimes the risks he took were unnecessary, like jumping through a window to escape when there were easier options, just to see if he could do it. Such exploits clearly echoed those of his childhood, when adventure, daring and danger were the permanent accompaniment to his inquisitive wanderings. At about the age of 15 or 16 and now a regular drinker, burglary became a central feature of Ron's life, with whole days being spent just thinking of somewhere to 'rob'. During this period, Ron got caught with an 18-year-old boy. They were tried in Crown Court. The older boy got detention, Ron a supervision order. His knees 'went' as it dawned on him that he could get done for things. But it didn't last. He'd now seen the worst: 'been there, seen it, done it', as he put it. All that happened was that he met a load of kids at the drop-in centre who introduced him to glue-sniffing.

Despite his bravado, Ron had not seen the worst. This came with the death of his cousin following a drunken ride on a motorbike they'd stolen. It crashed into a lamppost on the estate, killing the other boy, and leaving Ron feeling 'shit': unable to face people. He got 15 months' Borstal for reckless driving, as well as for some burglaries. Paroled after six months, he was still concerned about people's attitudes towards him when he came out. However, he had enjoyed his time inside, having met 'some right good kids there', and lapped up the educational courses on offer: 'If I'd 'ave been there longer I'd 'ave … just gone in every course what they 'ad.' In the event, his follow-up courses were to be a series of largely unsatisfactory youth training schemes (YTS). Though he enjoyed learning some new skills, like mechanics and catering, the constant moving from course to course, the lack of incentives ('I never got a certificate for doing owt'), and the 'crap' money eventually got to him. He ended up 'wagging it' to go glue-sniffing. He also fell out with some of the instructors. Once he 'flipped' when something was said about reckless driving ('I wanted to kill 'im and everything'); another time he 'flew off 'andle and … threatened to smack 'im' when he was made to look small after sticking up for a kid whom the instructor was picking on.

Apart from some time spent working away in fields, where the money was alright and you were left too 'knackered' to do anything else, and odd painting and decorating jobs for pensioners, Ron has not worked since. A couple of spells in bail hostels seemed to be less pleasant experiences than Borstal: 'I weren't right struck on them … there were a few dodgy kids in there.'

Though Ron showed little fear of concrete threats, like getting caught for burglary or injuring himself in daring escapades, he was afraid of more abstract threats, like nuclear war, global warming, and especially AIDS, about which he developed 'a right phobia'. Indeed, the thought of AIDS affected him so much that he gave up having sex for three years. But, even before the AIDS scare, as an amateur tattooist he had always been punctilious about needles and ink: 'I won't tattoo nobody twice. I wouldn't use same ink … Needles would get changed and sterilised and burnt and all sorts. It weren't just AIDS, it were owt.'

Whether it was becoming a father that did it, or simply 'growing out of crime', Ron's attitude to burglary has begun to change, evidenced in his conversion from burgling to 'scrapping'. A recent scrapping expedition that led to a burglary, partly because he was drunk ('which is my excuse'), led to him not venturing out for two days for fear of what people would think of him: 'I were thinking, fuckin' 'ell, people are gonna think I'm a right cunt going out burgling 'ouses round 'ere and that ... I'm more bothered about what people think than like getting caught ... Just right paranoid about it.' On another recent occasion, he took action against his cousin for stealing from people who were 'alright': 'I went mad. I beat me cousin up other week 'cos 'e'd ... nicked somebody's tent. And they're alright.' He went mad at his sister for trying to 'top herself', though others had advised him not to intervene.

He still takes risks. For example, he went on a scrapping expedition for electric cables which entailed sawing through a cable carrying 11,000 volts. It turned out to be live. This produced the loudest noise and the brightest light Ron had ever experienced. The flash left him running blind to escape and call the emergency services, thinking his mates were dead. The blindness lasted for an hour. It also left one of them with 40 per cent burns. There is none the less evidence that Ron is beginning to think more about his actions. On the scrapping expedition, Ron, who was usually to be found volunteering for the dangerous task, did not wield the saw, and was furthest back from the action. The incident has left him 'a bit worried now' and 'thinking daft things like what if it fuckin' just blew up, or ... summat', when hearing a buzzing coming from a cable they are thinking of pinching. On another occasion during the recent past, he needed assistance to get down from his roof on which he'd been fixing a CB aerial after he began thinking of what would happen if he caught his shoe. After years of climbing 'owt', extraordinary risk-taking and near catastrophic accidents, Ron froze, petrified: 'That were first time that I'd been ... really frightened of owt like that.' He also found himself unable to do a bungee jump as the operator was about to release him.

Other things have changed for Ron. The estate is not what it was. His friends have become 'smack-heads' who rob indiscriminately and inform on each other. His 'nutter' uncle is a heroin-addicted shadow of his former self. Ron enjoys using his punch bag. He'd like to get into his weights, but more often settles for getting stoned. He and his girlfriend let each other do their own thing, but he gets jealous when she visits the father of her first daughter. He's a bit frightened of being burgled, partly because he knows how easy it is to do so: he thinks the house he lives in now must have been burgled 30 times in all, seven times by him. Sometimes he races his car about like a 'fucking maniac'. He loves sleeping and dreaming: 'Some days ... I'll be in bed all fucking day ... Even when they're bad ... I'll go back into me dream and turn it around or summat.'[3]

Self, survival and safety

Given that our aim is to analyse and theorise Ron's relationship to his criminal activities, let us first clarify what assumptions we are working with about the self. In order to understand the development of self over a life, we have to ask how external reality impinges on and helps to constitute the self and also how internal reality recurrently has its effects. Internal reality is not a simple representation of external reality or the social world because of the workings of psychological processes such as fantasy, desire and defences against anxiety. Thus experience, being constituted from both external and internal reality, is simultaneously social and psychological (psychosocial), like the warp and weft of a piece of cloth. The complex way in which Ron's experience is psychosocial is the subject of our case analysis.

Remember that our basic theoretical premiss, following Klein, is that anxiety is inherent in the human condition. From this can follow an account of how social reality is transformed and made unique as it is internalised in the process of people experiencing events which are outside their boundaries and impinge on their selves. These experiences impinge on the basic safety of the self. According to Kleinian theory, the fear of personal annihilation is central to the earliest experience and this continues throughout life whenever anything unfamiliar is encountered (Hinshelwood, 1991: 219ff). If fear for the safety of the self were not a basic principle of life, how would a person's capacity to look after their own survival develop? This is a fundamental evolutionary principle. Klein therefore saw the death and life principles as instincts on which survival is based and therefore as fundamental premises of the self.

Yet human beings start off being dependent on others for their survival. This dependency covers both physical survival (food, warmth, shelter) and the subjective experience of both safety and threats to the self. From the start, therefore, external reality, usually in the shape of members of the immediate family, impinges on the internal experiences of danger and safety. Significant others can provide, or fail to provide, reliability in external conditions, containment and holding. By containment, we refer to Bion's argument (see Hinshelwood, 1991) that early threats to the self need to be contained by significant others who can 'detoxify' them by their own emotional survival and thus render them back in a transformed state. Winnicott's concept of holding (Hinshelwood, 1991) emphasises that physical holding is also a metaphor for psychological holding. It enables the infant to feel safe within its dependency on an object beyond itself. It is thus the basis of trust. The theme of safety can never be banished from a person's life and psychological development. A person's (largely unconscious) ways of coping with external threats to safety goes a long way in understanding who they are.

These early processes of self-development are highly relevant for an understanding of someone's biography. They establish the patterns of coping with threats, the meanings which attend people's responses to danger, risk and change in general. We know little about Ron's first few years. His parents lived together, his father was in employment, his sister was born when he was about two. We don't know when the parental rows started, nor exactly what violence Ron witnessed and what sense he was capable of making of it. When, later, he was sent to see a psychologist for fighting with his younger sister, he must have been seriously violent, given the norms of physical retribution in his family. His mother told him that it was probably because he had seen his father beat her up and was copying this behaviour. In psycho-analytic terms, he had internalised a violent relationship and, by iden-tifying with the (male) perpetrator, distanced himself (for protection) from the danger of victimisation. Either way, he was experiencing feel-ings of hate that he projected on to an external object.

Ron reckoned that 'summat right stressed me out when I were young ... about five or six or summat'. His destructive violence had extended to others outside his family and to himself. We can infer from his head-butting, his pulling his own hair out, his attack on a pupil with scissors, on another child with a brick, that his internal world was full of painful emotions which were being acted out in violent behav-iour to self and others. This internal world was already characterised by defences against anxiety operating to protect himself in the face of threatening external conditions.

What we have outlined here is the centrality of safety for the way in which the self develops; safety that includes both physical and psycho-logical dimensions. Safety produces feelings of security. Danger, its opposite, produces feelings of threat. Risk is the distance between dan-ger and safety, a distance defined by the self, its prowess, mastery and capacity to control the danger. The significance of risk in relation to both external (material and social) factors and to Ron's internal psycho-logical world is a central theme in our account.

Ron grew up in an environment which he could not depend upon. There were many moves between houses and family members after his parents broke up and he reiterated that nobody had ever told him and his sister what was happening. When his mum first left, he and his sister were with his dad for a short while. His mother had made him promise not to tell his dad where she'd gone, but he did. Then followed two years with his grandmother, then a move in with his mum and stepfather, where his mother's sister and her partner (the 'nutter' uncle whom he admired and identified with) also stayed for a while, sleep-ing on the floor. He hated his stepfather to the point of wanting to kill him. Ron and his sister moved in with their father again when he was about 13, for reasons that he can't remember (he thought he'd had a row with his mother), but it only lasted two weeks, when his father quickly discovered that Ron was beyond the reach of his authority.

A dependable home and dependable care signify psychological safety as well and Ron must have had to learn to do without those feelings of security. The carers were not dependable even though they were around. For example, when he was living with his grandmother, his father would buy him toys, but they would disappear. He reckons that his mum and/or stepfather sold them off when they needed ready cash, though he never knew for sure. This memory speaks of financial insecurity but also of a fundamental lack of trust: whether the suspicion was true or not, in his emotional life (represented in his memory), the adults whom he should most have been able to trust were responsible for stealing his possessions. Moreover, they were possessions that signified the continuing care of his father. (A later story about his stepfather cheating him over a motorcycle part suggests a continuation of the same untrustworthy relationship into Ron's teenage years.)

These were the years of Ron's 'attitude problem'. A necessary response to life-events that are incomprehensible, untrustworthy and uncontrollable is to protect the threatened self. Ron attempted to make himself invincible, to turn himself into the 'nutter' who ran the street: fearless, unpredictably violent, scary, and oblivious to consequences. To use terms you will by now be familiar with, we can say that Ron's anxieties about life changes he felt powerless to affect led to unconscious investment in available and protective practices deriving from the highly gendered discourse of the 'hardman'. In this, there is a special place for the 'crazy nutter' who is 'off his head', up for anything, willing to use violence with or without provocation, unmindful of consequences (see Collison, 1996; Jefferson, 1998).

To understand why the 'hard-man' discourse (and not some other way of acting out invincibility) comes to be the vehicle of his unconscious investment, we must attend to the social dimensions of Ron's life at the time. This is a young boy, remember, from a tough neighbourhood, who has been moved to his nan's, and has been forced to change schools. He thus has to re-establish himself on new streets and in a new school. When you don't arrive as part of a cohort, but are an isolated newcomer, this is particularly difficult. For boys in tough neighbourhoods, in particular, signs of weakness can easily lead to bullying; becoming accepted is partly about showing a willingness or an ability to stand up for yourself. It worked for Ron after he fought back when his milk was taken off him at his new school: 'they were alright, people after that' (he also mentions being 'right quiet' before that at his new school). Ron himself came to think that his attitude problem was linked to questions of acceptance: 'I think that might 'ave been what were up with me when I were younger, knows with swapping schools.' We know that he had similar difficulties settling in at his new secondary school; but then he took off, escaped to the countryside, rather than stay and fight for his place.

A more dramatic example occurred when Ron was nine or ten, after being bullied for two years by a bigger boy living close by. Encouraged by another boy to take the bully on, Ron knocked him to the floor, after which the 'relief on me mind were just unreal'. This, and similar incidents he witnessed subsequently, taught him that boys who act hard are not always what they seem: 'It's just how people bring them sen across to ya ... they just convince ya that they're just 'arder than ya, or summat ... or you convince yoursen.'

Once Ron had survived these early years, assisted no doubt by his regular escapes to the countryside (to which we return below), his use of violence, apart from incidents of 'flipping', seems more instrumental, more to do with social survival. The 'front' of the hard-man, as he learned from his childhood bully-neighbour, had to be more than just bluff. As Ron put it about survival in Borstal, everyone puts up a 'front', but 'when somebody calls your bluff ... then you've just got to fucking do it'. Ron's examples of responding with violence when he had been made to feel small fit within this category (a lad in the bail hostel; the YTS instructor who was picking on a smaller boy). The second of these examples also involved Ron sticking up for a smaller boy, a reason he likewise gave for once punching a bigger man in a pub. These two examples suggest that righting wrongs was also important, and not intended merely as a social message about Ron not being a man to be messed with.

Though these examples of Ron's instrumental use of violence are about 'front' and survival in a difficult social world where 'not taking shit' matters profoundly, they tend to happen when Ron is made to feel small or in defence of someone smaller or weaker, which is a position Ron can identify with from past experience. In short, even with that form of instrumental fighting most tied up with youthful masculine social identity, psychological as well as social survival is at stake for Ron. We also know that young Ron had a 'nutter' role model in his hardman-burglar uncle, who Ron looked up to because the uncle commanded respect through fear. So, for an emotionally disturbed boy having to establish street and school 'cred.' in a tough neighbourhood, and with a hardman live-in uncle for a role model, positioning as a 'nutter' made social as well as psychic sense: his choice was overdetermined.

Self-destructiveness can be part of the 'nutter' image, if done publicly, as a demonstration of one's obliviousness to pain or consequences or as part of a contest that Ron tried to initiate, as with head-butting walls. Even so, it is hard to see such obviously self-harming behaviours as having nothing to do with emotional disturbance of some kind. The literature on self-harm shows how physical pain can be a more bearable substitute for mental pain. It seems that Ron was testing his capacity to withstand physical pain, but in a situation where he was in control. By mastering physical pain, he could try to master mental pain. By being the hardest physically, he could convince himself that he could survive. His frequent use of 'not bothered' to mean not frightened by physical risks suggests a link between the physical and the mental: by being physically hard, he wouldn't bother or mind, that is not be upset in himself. 'Not bothered' also connotes an easy dismissal of something which has the power to upset you, thus implying having surmounted uncomfortable, perhaps painful, emotions.

However, these emotions sometimes burst through when Ron got so upset that he completely 'flipped', meaning that he became enraged and lost control of his actions, which were violent. He accounted for the scissors incident in these terms, though he no longer knew what the boy had done to deserve the stabbing. Later, he described his angry response to the YTS instructor in the same terms. 'Flipping' is not the same as being a 'nutter': the 'nutter' performs violence, to some extent cold-bloodedly, to instil fear; the 'flipper' might be said to be the person through whom violence is performed, despite himself, in the heat of the moment, once the red mist descends. If the 'nutter' is 'not bothered' about the consequences of his actions, the person who 'flips' is clearly very bothered about something, as Ron was when the YTS instructor stirred up painful emotions around his cousin's death. The threat to his safety that bothered Ron on this and other occasions when he 'flipped' was internal, not external; a threat to his self, not a danger to his body.

From being dependent on a family which let him down, on which he could not rely, Ron became independent at a very young age: 'I brought mesen up.' We know that Ron only ever had money or new clothes when he acquired them himself – through thieving. He thus took responsibility for catering for his own needs through crime. As soon as he was able, Ron escaped and explored the unknown, at every opportunity. His earliest associations in the first interview were to the pleasure of adventurousness with an older friend, far away from his family and neighbourhood, out in the country. This older boy may have been the person Ron most trusted in the world. His slippages into the present tense suggest the continuing emotional significance of this relationship:

> *Ron:* like from being young and that wi' going out wi' 'im, 'e like fucking brought me up more, you know … I grew up to, like, even when I'm frightened of doing things and that, I fucking, I knew like 'e wouldn't let me down or owt, you know? I could trust 'im and that. 'E could pull me up a fucking big wall or summat like that, or a roof or summat

[*Tony*: Yeah] and I – thinking that I were gonna fall. So long as like I thought 'e were there and 'e were gonna fucking 'elp me, I know I was gonna be alright, do you know what I mean?

They mastered unfamiliar surroundings by taking risks, extending their physical capacities: running, climbing, breaking and entering, and, for Ron, this all took place in the context of being able to put his trust in another person. Ron makes a link also between risk and being in control in the context of a recent example where he was driving 'like a fucking maniac ... thinking that I'm in control'. (He endangered his own and his girlfriend's life when the movements of another car made his own driving control almost irrelevant.) The elation of risk here is connected to control: risk is a threat that can be turned into a narcissistic triumph by mastery. This way, one can recurrently prove capable of protecting the self against annihilation.

By his physical and fighting prowess, Ron achieved some control over an external world which was unsafe in a great many respects. Exerting control over his internal world was a different matter and there is a mass of evidence which points to this being a persistent problem for Ron. While the young Ron was invincible by day, with his tough guy defences in place, at night, with his unconscious anxiety at the helm, the nightmares returned. They were about Ron's inability to defend himself from the threat of poisoning.

We were alerted to this through the evidence Ron supplied about his risk-taking. On the one hand, there were a whole series of physical risks which he tried to control (usually successfully) through physical prowess; on the other, he talked of fears about the risks involved in smoking, sex, dirty needles and taking pills. Ron pointed to the significance of the distinction with his own associations about the different categories. The risks that he avoids are about 'owt what goes into me body'. The former category of risks, which permit recurrent mastery of the external world, result, in contrast, in 'surface wounds, you know cuts to skin and things'. The skin forms the boundary between the external and internal world. As long as the risks to Ron did not go beyond the surface, his self was not threatened. If, on the other hand, the danger could get inside, then the self would be threatened.

The evidence that this was the case comes from Ron's phobias. A phobia (Ron's word) is an irrational fear, displaced from its real source, which we are arguing is the fear of annihilation. There are, of course, real dangers in dirty tattooing needles or unprotected sex, or smoking. Ron was aware of these. For example, several of his older relatives had died of cancer and in prison he had been exposed to a lot of information about HIV transmission. These are the external realities. But the realistic response to the fear of AIDS transmission is to wear a condom, not to abstain from sex for several years. 'But it weren't just AIDS it were owt.' In his inner reality, with his history of never being able to internalise safety from the outside, he suffered paranoid anxieties about contaminating his insides – even with a headache pill. In Kleinian theory, as a defence against anxiety, good and bad (safety and danger in this example) are split off from each other. The danger can be projected out, to keep what is inside free from its badness. The environment then, in fantasy, holds a series of risks which always threaten to get back inside where the danger originally resided. These are the dangers that Ron cannot master through physical prowess. They have in common the theme of contamination, of something bad getting inside.

Following from things getting inside his body, Ron's next association was one that he had not anticipated:

> *Ron:* It weren't just AIDS, it were owt. [*Tony:* Mmm.] There was that, oh fucking 'ell, going back to when I were right young, I used to 'ave – I used to be frightened of being poisoned or summat for some reason … nightmares that … I were gonna die because I'd been poisoned and one day … I used to 'ave dreams that I'd got chocolate bars and I'd ate 'alf way through 'em … and I'd notice fucking spiders' legs or summat … And I knew it weren't right and one day I got offered … I were with me nan … normally I would – owt for nowt – would 'ave 'ad it and then I thought, like I don't know this person … They might be just trying to poison me or summat. I were about six.

A memory from his childhood erupted into consciousness, signalled by the dreamlike and surprised quality in his voice. He 'knew it weren't right'; that is, he knew he was not being realistic. This is what characterises paranoid anxieties. These nightmares illustrate the symbolic power of the metaphor of ingestion. Not to take in food is to die, but how is one to separate the good (the chocolate bar) from the bad (the spiders' legs) so as to avoid the annihilation of being poisoned?

Psychoanalysts have pointed out a similar dilemma for men engaging in penetrative heterosexual sex, a dilemma summed up in the image of *vagina dentata*. The defining difference between the sexes, arguably far more basic than girls' 'lack' of a penis, is that while men's genitals are on the surface, women's vaginas are internal. This distinction mirrors Ron's splitting of dangers into two kinds, the surface kind that he's 'not bothered' by and the inside kind that he fears and cannot control. Ron explained why having sex with his girlfriend didn't worry him, after his previous fears of AIDS and consequent sexual abstinence, by using the phrase 'I've been there, 'aven't I?' The pronoun implies that he (his self) goes into this internal place. Now it is safe because it is familiar, but it suggests that, for a while, he was reluctant to have sex, not because of AIDS, but because of risking going inside (into the 'female' world of emotions, back into dependency) where before he could try to live on the surface.

Adventure, curiosity and burglary

Criminological explanations of Ron's turn to burglary would emphasise the social features and miss the psychic importance to Ron of
curiosity.[4] And it is true that his chaotic family life, the criminal role
models, the high-crime neighbourhood, his poverty, truanting, lack of
qualifications and unemployment are part of Ron's story and cannot be
ignored. After all, Ron is an underclass male child of the harsh socio-
economic climate that was Thatcherism. But a purely social explanation will not do. He did avoid the heroin-addicted fate of many of his
mates (perhaps because of his fear of injecting poisonous substances).
Curiosity, a desire for adventure and going on trips to the countryside
are not unusual, perhaps especially for a multiply-deprived urban boy
child like Ron. But Ron's earliest associations to adventure invoke
more, namely, the lure of danger. Mastery is part of growing up, especially for many young boys, deeply embedded in codes of masculinity.
For working-class youngsters, lacking the carefully monitored envi-
ronments of the middle-class child, adventures will be wilder, less controlled, more dangerous. But we still have to confront Ron's attraction
to danger, the way he ignored even extreme warnings on finds that he
liked to examine: 'toxic, fucking poisonous'. It had a compulsive feel to
it, of a force emanating from another place, as Ron himself recognised
('I 'ad to'). It is this compulsiveness that makes us doubt the sufficiency
of a purely discursive explanation; namely, that mischievous boys are
attracted to danger because it enhances their dare-devil reputation in
the tough/hard school of masculinity. If, in ignoring danger signs, Ron
is taking up an available position in a gender-differentiated discourse
which enhances his masculinity and thus his self-esteem as a boy, this
can hardly explain a boy being moved to put his hands in holes, a compulsion which seems connected to a wider fascination to going inside,
entering things.

Ron's fascination with going inside protected or prohibited places
goes right back to when he started collecting keys,[5] which was before
their utilitarian value in burgling. In the manner of free association to
events that the narrative interview method is designed to elicit, Ron
associated from entering houses or barns, the interviewer's original
question, to putting his hands in tree-holes as an example of 'if I saw
summat, I 'ad to examine it' (the word 'examine' connoting detailed
and close attention). This theme of entering cropped up again and
again in the interviews – often in connection with keys.[6] The example
of putting his ' 'ands in 'oles' casts the earlier 'I just 'ad to go in and
'ave a look' in a more psychodynamic light: something compelled him
to enter and examine – houses, holes. In other words, the motivation
that we are positing for Ron's curiosity and adventurousness derives
from unconscious forces: he is compelled but there is no reason for it

that he can comprehend. The key represents the resource to get inside somewhere that is not automatically accessible. It suggests that the results of Ron's early experiences of psychological unsafety, and particularly perhaps his lack of an experience of a place (home) inside which he could feel safe, were carried with him in the compulsion to get inside, whether it was putting his hands in holes or opening doors with keys, or breaking and entering. Physically, he could master these spaces but, psychologically, their danger came back to haunt him in the shape of spiders' legs in chocolate bars and HIV in vaginas.

This compulsion to enter dangerous places is thus the flipside of his fear of things entering him: to be the one who enters potentially dangerous spaces is to test out one's power or control by risking danger, as we saw earlier. The psychoanalyst Riviere maintains this very point:

> [love of power] derives from the attempt to control the dangers in oneself more directly than by the methods of projection and of flight ... one way of reaching security is by aiming at omnipotent power in order to control all potentially painful conditions ... one form of omnipotence as a means of obtaining security consists in experimenting, as it were, with danger, in order to test one's power of escape. (Riviere, 1964: 39)

While this interpretation stresses Ron's relation to his internal reality, external reality was affected by his actions. The first burglary netted £40. For a youngster like Ron, who had never had any money, bringing himself up with little help from his mother and forced to wear hand-me-down jeans from his female cousin, the feeling of having money must have been liberatory. And, as he got older, and his liking for (and need of) money grew, the instrumental reasons for burglary, for someone in Ron's social position and from his background, no doubt begin to exert their own social 'compulsion'. But, to stop there is to miss another important element of these early burglary expeditions: their connection to risk. Ron explained it in terms of wanting to 'get involved', as in the following example:

> *Ron:*   I suppose I like – I like to get involved a lot. If – if, if we're robbing summat and only way in's a fucking 'igh window or summat, I'll be one who's fucking put me 'and up and say [*Tony*: Yeah] d'y'know, 'I'll, I'll climb up' and that. And I'll go along fucking asbestos roof and that. [*Tony*: Yeah.] Take chances of falling 20 foot through building or summat, you know?

One reading of Ron's apparent willingness to be the one to take risks on behalf of the group contemplating burglary would emphasise discursive positioning: the heightened esteem within his (all male) peer group of partners-in-crime which would accrue, especially when done on behalf of the group. But this does not explain Ron jumping through windows to escape, when 'there were no need for it', as in the following extract:

> *Ron:* Once – we were once in empty 'ouses, that what were there, can't remember 'ow old they were. Closed road off and that. Er, I think we were nicking some – a bit of cut lead or summat off roofs. Summat daft. We were inside this 'ouse and coppers come, and they come to front, and like I jumped up on window ledge and jumped up and it were, it were cracked window anyway – but jumped straight through it and landed in front garden and run off. And this kid like followed me, and it were only empty 'ouses like. There were no need for it. It were just, know what I mean? I could 'ave just got out of back or summat I suppose. I think I 'ad it in me 'ead that I were going – just gonna do it just to see if I could do it.

Here, Ron's risk-taking, though undoubtedly masculinity accomplishing, also has an irrational, compulsive dimension too (like "'ands in 'oles'), one for which a purely social explanation is inadequate. His physical mastery was tested and proved beyond the risks posed by the actual situation.

Ron was 'not bothered' when he had an attitude problem and he was 'not bothered' about being caught for burglary. Indeed, far from being bothered, he talked of collapsing into helpless laughter when being chased. Such sentiments, about having a laugh and not bothering, are recognisable features of a certain form of class masculinity as Willis (1977) evocatively charted. But with Ron there are clear echoes of the disdainful invincibility that characterised his 'nutter' years; and, just as we argued there about the defensive function of that invincible front, its defensive function here should not be overlooked. Once again, the need for a psychosocial explanation of Ron's behaviour becomes evident.

Thieving, fighting and morality

While earlier in his life, Ron was living on the edge, sometimes risking death in a way that seems almost compulsive, lately he is more cautious and takes more care of himself and others. In these changes, we can explore the connections between risk and morality and the self. For example, Ron's phobias about taking things inside his body can also be seen as caring for his body and himself. He tries not to drink too much alcohol because 'I'm funny na, about 'ow much I drink and that … If I feel shit next day I know that it's fucking 'cos me body rejecting it and all that, do you know?'

Let us start with the aspects of Ron's criminal activities that can most superficially be viewed as immoral. First, he harms people physically; secondly, he takes things that belong to other people. Yet in both of these areas he operates moral judgements, even if his behaviour is not always consistent with these principles. As he moved from stealing keys from empty places to stealing for money and goods to be fenced, Ron and his peers adopted the local ethic that you don't steal from those you know. At first he did not burgle on his own estate for this reason, although freely admitting that he would do so on a different estate where the people were no different. Later on they needed the money. Even then, they distinguished between people who were 'alright' and the others. Ron tries to teach others, like his cousin, this principle, by beating him up. While physical violence might seem wholly immoral to some, Ron uses it to teach moral lessons and does not question this link between violence and morality. These are examples of taking on board a moral principle which is shared in a certain community, a kind of social learning of morality, although it did not work very reliably. He claims that 'There's only so far I can go.' There is an attractive discursive position here – moral limits to his criminal activity – in which he can cast himself in a relatively favourable light.

However, this does not explain what psychological processes were involved in Ron's actions when he desisted from stealing. From the associations in his narrative, two psychological principles were apparent: trust and identification with the victim.

> *Ron:* So when I've robbed owt, when I, even when we used to go out robbing and that, from being kids. If we got in a church summat like that, nowt got took. Do you know what I mean? [*Tony*: Mmm.] I once seen a cash box full of notes, I pulled screws off wall and everything, I were gonna take it and we didn't. But it were right, it were just weird 'ow it 'appened that. 'Cos we were down [the name of a country village] and it pissed it down wi' rain and there were fucking, we were like middle of nowhere and we got to this thing and there were a gate on this like vicarage thing. And it 'ad key on it for church. It says like, key to church and all that, took it. Whatever. We went and sat in church till we dried out. Had us sandwiches and that there. And that's when we seen money. We were gonna take it and that. I says 'No, can't take it' 'cos fucking, do you know what I mean? They'd fucking, they'd trusted us like. [*Tony*: Yeah.] Left us key and everything.
> *Tony:* Yeah. Yeah. So that affected you? The fact that they trusted you?
> *Ron:* Mmm. Like if I ever – if I ever burgle anybody's 'ouse I never go in kid's room, do you know what I mean? Never touch owt like that. Never take, er, I took money off sides like. Big jars, but I've never like a kid's money box or owt, do you know what I mean? [*Tony*: Yeah.] Or burgled old people or owt.

This extract starts with 'so', which refers back to what came immediately before. One of the dangers with extracts is of losing the sequence and thus the *Gestalt* within which they derive their fuller meaning. Ron uses 'so' to contrast his own robbing with that of the man he had met in a probation hostel who had been convicted for aggravated burglary. 'I didn't agree with it, that is with burglary victims being beaten up. So when I've robbed owt ...' He doesn't complete this train of thought, which presumably would have continued 'I've never beaten anybody up.' Instead, his association is to a particular day when he could have robbed a church. In this example, no one is directly at risk of being beaten up. The association is one suggesting a different or wider morality.

This is quite a long story for Ron in the interview context, with an unusual amount of vivid scene-setting. It was 'pissing down' with rain, they were very wet and in the middle of nowhere. On a gate near the vicarage, a key was provided with a notice inviting anyone to use it to enter the church. They dried off and ate their sandwiches: in other words, they took shelter. Then they saw the money: 'a cash box full of notes' and Ron got as far as pulling the screws out of the wall. For the second time Ron explains that they didn't take the money.[7] That the key was offered to be taken legitimately meant to Ron that somebody trusted him, had provided shelter when he needed it, and therefore he would not betray that trust.

His next association to trust is that of not taking children's money boxes or going into children's bedrooms. He is positioning himself as someone who children can trust. We know that Ron remembers never having had any money when he was a child unless he stole it. We also know that he believed that either his mother or stepfather stole his toys when young. This time (unlike when he fought his sister as a younger boy) he identified with the potential victim and, in protecting the child victim, experienced a different safety from that of the 'nutter' or hard-man. In these two examples, the relational, or intersubjective, aspect of subjectivity is illustrated, first consciously and then unconsciously. In the church example, Ron finds himself positioned (impersonally) as trustworthy and he acts accordingly. In the children example, he positions himself as trustworthy, but to do this he must have projected his own vulnerability into the child(ren) and identified with it there, thus not treating them along with most categories of people, whose potential vulnerability he did not identify with. Later, he was trustworthy with old people, not stealing from them if he went to do a decorating job.

Recently, Ron found himself in a difficult moral dilemma. They broke into a securely boarded house on the estate where he knew there was some scrap metal to steal. Once inside, much to their surprise, they found video, TV and all the signs of someone having just moved in. They didn't even know if the house was occupied. Ron felt uncomfortable, but they proceeded to take out everything of value. His reasoning was that, if they were caught, they'd be done for burglary whether they'd taken everything or not: 'I'd have been a fool to mesen.' But, as we saw, he did not venture out for two days for fear of what people would think of him: 'I'm more bothered about what people think than like getting caught … Just right paranoid about it.' In other words, he felt shame. The psychological process involved is one where Ron is able to put himself in another's position and feel ashamed at what the other person would feel about him. He sounds puzzled at experiencing this more strongly than the fear usually associated with the prospect of a prison sentence.

This suggests that Ron's capacities for identification are developing. He gives some examples which do not relate to his criminal activities as well. For example, he is concerned about global warming and those dying of famine in Africa. More practically, he gives blood (though doing so precipitated a paranoid fear that the two-week silence meant that he was HIV positive). He was extremely concerned for his partner when she was pregnant and also for the safety of his baby. It was not clear if this was more worry than care since he did not get involved in the day-to-day care of the baby.

He took a different kind of risk after his sister attempted suicide, trying to tell her that she must not think of doing so again, despite advice that he would make it worse: 'So I just went in and said "Look, don't be fucking stupid … if tha wants to do it, fucking don't fucking like, tha not fucking 'urting thee, tha 'urting everybody else." ' A path of identification is suggested here. His sister was suicidal because she felt responsible for the death of a boyfriend (one of Ron's friends). She had started seeing him when her earlier boyfriend was in gaol, but when this man had come out, he had stabbed and killed the other man. Ron too had felt 'shit' when his cousin had been killed on the stolen bike they were riding together. He might have known the temptation to take one's own life, but he had not succumbed.

In Kleinian theory, the capacity to position oneself in relation to both self and others, to exhibit concern for others and to recognise the self's capacity to do harm to others are seen as central to the development of self within primary relationships. In Ron's case we have cited examples of how these capacities are the condition for moral judgements which bear upon his criminal activities.

There is widespread comment on the perceived empirical connection between deprived and disturbed family backgrounds and boys' delinquency and crime. However, usually the connection is talked of as if adults failed to model moral behaviour and, in particular, failed to impose strict enough sanctions on their children. While both of these were partly true in Ron's case, we do not believe that this social learning model of morality grasps the unconscious emotional processes through which he first became a violent and harmful 'nutter' and later extended his identifications with vulnerable people in such a way that he started to want to protect them. His moral relationship to the harsh social world he encountered as a child was defined by these psychological processes.

Memory, reality and truth

Our application of Kleinian psychoanalytic principles sees remembering as a process in continual tension between a truthful acknowledgement of the (emotional) reality of a past event and defensive distortions of that reality in the service of psychological self-protection. Ron's account (here pared down) of the motorbike accident in which his cousin was killed is a telling illustration of the tension surrounding the remembering of a painful and anxiety-provoking event. Ron volunteered this account in response to Tony asking him whether there was an event that 'bothered' him (in the context of Ron frequently saying he wasn't bothered): 'We nicked a bike, drunk ... had a crash on it ... and 'e died ... I felt shit ... I got 15 month for it ... reckless driving.' He could have avoided relating the incident at all, or he could have claimed that his cousin was driving the bike (as, so we heard from a different interviewee, he had done immediately after the event). He did neither. However, his account demonstrates some ambivalence in the indirect way the interviewer is told that Ron was driving. Although he does not state his responsibility outright, neither does he conceal it. In this example, the Kleinian concepts of paranoid-schizoid and depressive functioning provide a yardstick for assessing how reality-based Ron's account is: with difficulty he bears the revelation of a painful truth in this encounter. This is an example of maintaining depressive position functioning, rather than resorting to paranoid-schizoid splitting to deny the reality. Based on the preservation of the whole of the data, it is also possible to assess a claim in the account in the light of other parts of the data and their relation to the whole. For example, if we were in any doubt about Ron's claim to have been 'bothered' by the motorbike accident, we would be convinced by the account, offered in a different thematic context, of how he 'flipped' and hit out at a training instructor for saying something about reckless driving.

Remembering something more or less truthfully is not, in this view, an achievement which is located solely within the individual. It has two sources: one in an individual's biography; the other in the inter-subjective dynamics surrounding the telling. Memory works biographically in the sense that earlier events are reworked in the light of later meanings (Scott, 1996). There is no unmediated version of the original event. However, reality still makes a claim on memory: the denial of what really happened requires the continual application of defensive energies. It is easy to imagine how much Ron would like to believe that he was not the driver of the bike at the time of the accident. Under certain circumstances, he might have come to 'remember' it being the other way round, as a way of coping with an unbearable reality. However, he is able to tell a story which is truthful in this basic respect.

Ron's account was elicited in the particular context of the interview relationship: the account he provided was a function of the intersubjective conditions of the moment. In Chapter 3, we introduced the concepts of recognition and containment to theorise some important aspects of the unconscious intersubjective dynamics that may make it possible to tell a story that is potentially threatening to the self. How the story is recognised, contained and respected points to a different principle for research ethics than principles of informed consent. We hope to have illustrated in this chapter a recognising, containing and respectful relationship to Ron and his account.

We have also stressed the co-production of any research account in the sense that the interviewer's meanings and defences are implicated in the production and analysis of data. This does not mean that the account is not the interviewee's story, however. The research relationship is clearly structured to distinguish between teller and listener. The structure and the principles of free-association narrative interviewing maximise the possibility of a rich and relatively truthful story being told (note that they do not guarantee it). The telling is a product of a unique moment and relationship (another time it would come out differently) and, at the same time, it bears a relationship to actual events which, using the principles of defended subjects and their variable relationships to reality, can be deciphered.

The 'order' of free associations

The free-association narrative interview method is based on the premiss that the meanings underlying interviewees' elicited narratives are best accessed via links based on spontaneous association, rather than whatever consistency can be found in the told narrative. This is a radically different conception of meaning because free associations follow an emotional rather than a cognitively derived logic. Once we follow that logic, the result is a fuller picture than would otherwise have emerged, offering richer and deeper insights into a person's unique meanings. Take as an example Ron's association from AIDS to his nightmares of being poisoned. It is an unprompted link that seems to surprise him. He is about to continue with his story about AIDS, but pauses, then utters, in a dramatically different, lower, almost dream-like, tone of voice, 'oh fucking 'ell.'

By attending to the apparently incoherent links Ron makes at this point in the transcript, we made a connection that followed an emotional logic, namely, the 'irrational' fear of things getting inside him common to Ron's relationship to AIDS and to the chocolate bars or crisps he imagined to be poisoned. From seeing the logic of his free association, we interpreted the anxiety underpinning both. That gave us more insight into an apparent contradiction: the ways in which this paranoid feeling of inner unsafety coexisted with the (apparently) invulnerable exterior of Ron the risk-taker. In other words, being attentive to the emotional logic provided by Ron's association enabled us to make more sense not only of his relation to AIDS and poisoning, but also of his reckless risk-taking.

This is an example of an account which began in a way that was structured according to a principle of narrative progression and was transformed by the spontaneous emergence of a memory into awareness. The account at this point is structured according to the principle of free association, dictated by unconscious rather than conscious logic.[8] Our method aims to facilitate moves from the former to the latter, in the belief that researchers' understanding of experience, meaning and identity will be enriched. It gives priority to the meanings inherent in the links, rather than the meanings contained within statements. In the interstices, we believe, is revealed a subject beyond the unitary, rational subject of most social science.

Summary

- Our own relationships, as researchers, to Ron and to crime, were explored to see how they might have affected the interview dynamics and data analysis.
- We provided a detailed pen portrait of Ron, the aim of which was to give the reader a descriptive summary of the information from our two interviews with him.
- We outlined a theory of how a self develops, emphasising the need for psychological security and the coping mechanisms used when the external world does not provide safety, reliability and the basis for trust.
- We interpreted Ron's investment in risk-taking and burglary psychosocially, taking account of his demographic position, discourses of masculinity and the psychological need to master danger. We demonstrated how he split off risks to the body into inside, which he experienced as dangerous, and outside, which he felt able to control.
- We drew upon Kleinian and social analyses to understand Ron's moral relationship to his criminal activities.
- We used Ron's recollection of a tragic incident in which he was implicated to discuss and theorise interviewees' capacities for remembering truthfully.
- Ron's recall of a childhood incident provided a final example of eliciting emotionally – rather than cognitively – derived associations and the assistance this provided in understanding more fully Ron's relationship to crime.

Notes

1   For a contrasting, purely social case study of a career burglar conducted in the 'tell it like it is' research tradition, see Maguire (1982: Ch. 4).

2   This is not to suggest that the 'typical' burglary is necessarily 'nasty'; just that the experience of being burgled is frightening for the majority of people (Maguire, 1982: 133).

3   This comment also suggests the importance to Ron of mastery or control over dangerous situations, even if they are not real ones.

4   Walsh (1980: 62) and Bennett and Wright (1984: 133–40) notice the importance of excitement to some burglars, but fail to interpret it, while Wright and Decker's interpretation (1994: 56–8) is very brief, albeit suggestive.

5   Ron also collected (stole) birds' eggs – a symbol of where life begins, inside a protective shell.

6   Ron's first memory of robbing anything is breaking into a council hut because 'I'd got it into my head that they kept spare keys for 'ouses in this 'ut'.

7   Ron's shifts between 'I' and 'we' in this story are revealing. At first it sounds as if another boy desisted ('I were gonna take it and we didn't'). Next time round, Ron claims responsibility for the restraint, even putting it in direct speech. Either way, they did not and Ron internalised the moral principle. It is likely he was with the trusted older friend and was prepared to hear about trust from someone he trusted.

8   A thematically based attempt to make sense of Ron's narrative would have missed this because it would have sorted and coded all the references to AIDS in order to make sense of them, then all the references to nightmares, and so on.

AFTERWORD

In this book we have advocated a method of qualitative research which we believe makes a difference to the knowledge that social science is capable of producing. The free-association narrative interview method is not a substitute for all qualitative methods and is not appropriate for all types of research question. It is most powerful when the research question involves understanding people's experiences through their own meaning-frame and when the area that needs to be tapped to address the research question implicates a person's sense of self. In our view, this includes – or should include – a very broad terrain. The principles of a defended subject are very widely applicable to social research, but these principles have a particular contribution to make to interviewing methods. This is because interviewing based on the question-and-answer method is so influential in eliciting from the interviewee thin, rationally driven accounts which leave out more than they allow of human subjects.

Take the research into the fear of crime. Where do the narrow stereotypes of the fearful older woman or the fearless young man come from? In our particular example, the primary definitions of the fear of crime are delivered by the bi-annual British Crime Survey, in the form of the statistical aggregations of the answers to their question 'How safe do you feel, etc.?' Put bluntly, the fearful older woman is, at base, a depleted product of a depleted method. The fact that such a caricature may become a self-fulfilling prophesy, as elderly women identify with the media stereotypes offered up in their name, adds irony to insult. Since question-and-answer interview methods are widespread, even within the qualitative tradition, it follows that the vision of human subjects upon which key users of research, such as policy-makers and governments rely, is a depleted one. This is not only bad for policy but insulting to people.

Being able to offer an enriched, more complex, nuanced and, arguably, more humane and ethical view of the human subject could, then, be the biggest single difference that can be made by adopting our method. We hope that our illustrative glimpses of human subjects have respected this complexity: people's struggles with the constraints and possibilities of their social circumstances; their unique biographies; their creative capacities; their ethical impulses and the conditions which compromise these impulses; the vulnerability but also the robustness of human psyches in the face of painful, sometimes unbearable assaults on psychological survival. To the extent that these portraits have captured something of the complexity of our subjects, they can be said to be 'truer'; and, to that extent, more humane and ethical accounts.

In capturing something of the complexity of our subjects, we offer something true about them. In this respect, our method is different from most contemporary approaches in that it is neither relativist nor constructionist. The discursive turn has been valuable in disrupting the traditional idea of the transparent, unmediated self, but it renders issues of the (relative) honesty and truth in research accounts impossible to grasp. We hope that our approach stops short of throwing out the baby of truth with the bathwater of certainty, and can hang on to sociological insights without reducing our subjects to such merely social determinants.

The changes we are advocating – recognising the role of defences against anxiety in mediating our relationship to reality, the importance of unconscious intersubjectivity, and how free associations can give access to a post-rational unitary subject – are quite small, but the effect of their widespread adoption in qualitative research could be very big. Layers of meaning and experience to which research (and hence policy-makers) have rarely had access would become visible. The human subjects of research might be represented with the complexity we currently associate with literature and works of art more generally. This book is a demonstration of a method that moves in this direction.

APPENDIX: PRO FORMA

One pro forma (two sides of A4 paper) was filled in for each interviewee as part of the case analysis.

Case summary

1 Initials
 (interviewee/interviewer)

2 Location

3 Age

4 Sex

5 Race

6 Employment

7 Marital status
 (history)

8 Family
 (history)

9 Children/grandchildren

10 Health
 (history)

11 Criminal victimisation
 (history)

12 Fear of crime
 (history)

13 At risk/risk-taking
 (history)   [self report:]

14 Anxiety/worry/traumatic events
 (history)   [self report:]

15 Interviewer/interviewee relationship

16 Other comments/themes/summary

REFERENCES

Abbott, A. (1992) 'What do cases do? Some notes on activity in sociological analysis', in C. Ragin and H. Becker (eds), *What is a Case? Exploring the Foundations of Social Inquiry*. New York: Cambridge University Press. pp. 53–82.

Alderson, P. (1998) 'Confidentiality and consent in qualitative research', *BSA Network*, 69: 6–7.

Alvarez, A. (1985) 'The problem of neutrality', *Journal of Child Psychotherapy*, 11: 87–103.

Aron, L. (1996) *The Meeting of Minds*. Hillsdale, NJ: Analytic Press.

Bauer, Martin (1996) 'The narrative interview', *LSE Methodology Institute Papers*, Qualitative Series, No. 1.

Benjamin, J. (1995) *Like Subjects, Love Objects*. New Haven, CT and London: Yale University Press.

Bennett, T. and Wright, R. (1984) *Burglars on Burglary: Prevention and the Offender*. Aldershot: Gower.

Berg, D.N. and Smith, K.K. (eds) (1988) *The Self in Social Inquiry: Researching Methods*. Newbury Park, CA: Sage.

Bion, W. (1984) *Learning from Experience*, 2nd edn (first published 1962). London: Maresfield.

Bowlby, J. (1970/1) 'Reasonable fear and natural fear: a critical evaluation', *International Journal of Psychiatry*, 9: 79–88.

British Psychological Society (1996) *Code of Conduct, Ethical Principles and Guidelines*. Leicester: BPS Press.

British Sociological Association (1996) *Statement of Ethical Practice*. Durham: BSA Publications.

Bunge, M. (1993) 'Realism and antirealism in social science', *Theory and Decisions*, 35: 207–35.

Chase, S.E. (1995) 'Taking narrative seriously: consequences for method and theory in interview studies', in R. Josselson and A. Lieblich (eds), *The Narrative Study of Lives*, Vol. 3. London: Sage. pp. 1–26.

Coffey, A. and Atkinson, P. (1996) *Making Sense of Qualitative Data*. London: Sage.

Collison, M. (1996) 'In search of the high life: drugs, crime, masculinities and consumption', *British Journal of Criminology*, 36 (3): 428–44.

Currie, D. and MacLean, B. (1997) 'Measuring violence against women: the interview as a gendered social encounter', in M.D. Schwartz (ed.), *Researching Sexual Violence Against Women: Methodological and Personal Perspectives*. Thousand Oaks, CA: Sage. pp. 157–78.

Day Sclater, S. (1998) 'Creating the self: stories as transitional phenomena', *Auto/biography*, 6: 85–920.

Denzin, N. (1989) *Interpretive Interactionism*. Newbury Park, CA: Sage.

Devereux, G. (1967) *From Anxiety to Method in the Behavioural Sciences*. The Hague: Mouton.

Douglas, M. (1986) *Risk Acceptability according to the Social Sciences*. London: Routledge and Kegan Paul.

Edelson, M. (1988) 'The hermeneutic turn and the single case study in psychoanalysis', in D.N. Berg and K.K. Smith (eds), *The Self in Social Inquiry: Researching Methods*. Newbury Park, CA: Sage. pp. 71–104.

Ernst, S. (1997) 'Mothers and daughters in a changing world', in W. Hollway and B. Featherstone (eds), *Mothering and Ambivalence*. London: Routledge. pp. 80–8.

Farrell, S., Bannister, J., Ditton, J. and Gilchrist, E. (1997) 'Questioning the measurement of the "fear of crime"', *British Journal of Criminology*, 37 (4): 658–79.

Ferraro, K.F. (1995) *Fear of Crime: Interpreting Victimization Risk*. New York: SUNY Press.

Ferraro, K.F. and LaGrange, R. (1987) 'The measurement of fear of crime', *Sociological Inquiry*, 57 (1): 70–101.

Freud, S. (1938) 'Splitting of the ego in the defensive process', *The Standard Edition of the Works of Sigmund Freud*, ed. James Strachey, Vol. 23. London: Hogarth Press. pp. 271–8.

Gilchrist, E., Bannister, J., Ditton, J. and Farrell, S. (1998) 'Women and the "fear of crime": challenging the accepted stereotype', *British Journal of Criminology*, 38 (2): 283–98.

Heimann, P. (1950) 'On counter-transference', *International Journal of Psycho-Analysis*, 31: 81–4.

Henriques, J., Hollway, W., Urwin, C., Venn, C. and Walkerdine, V. (1998) *Changing the Subject: Psychology, Social Regulation and Subjectivity*, 2nd edn (first published 1984). London: Routledge.

Hinshelwood, R.D. (1991) *A Dictionary of Kleinian Thought*. London: Free Association Books.

Hinshelwood, R.D. (1997) *Therapy or Coercion?* London: Karnac.

Hollway, W. (1989) *Subjectivity and Method in Psychology*. London: Sage.

Hollway, W. (1999) 'Take the violent toys from the boys?: Desire for containment and the containment of desire', *Child and Clinical Psychology and Psychiatry*, 4 (2): 277–82.

Hollway, W. and Jefferson, T. (1997) 'Eliciting narrative through the in-depth interview', *Qualitative Inquiry*, 3 (1): 53–70.

Hollway, W. and Jefferson, T. (1998) ' "A kiss is just a kiss": date rape, gender and contradictory subjectivities', *Sexualities*, 1 (4): 405–24.

Hollway, W. and Jefferson, T. (1999) 'Gender, generation, anxiety and the reproduction of culture: a family case study', in R. Josselson and A. Lieblich (eds), *The Narrative Study of Lives*, Vol. 6. London: Sage. pp. 107–39.

Hollway, W. and Jefferson, T. (2000) 'Narrative discourse and the unconscious: a case study of Tommy', in M. Andrews, S. Day Sclater, C. Squire and A. Treacher (eds), *Lines of Narrative*. London: Routledge.

Hollway, W. and Jefferson, T. (unpublished) 'How one heterosexual couple copes with fear of crime'.

Home Office Standing Conference on Crime Prevention (1989) *Report of the Working Group on the Fear of Crime*. London: Home Office.

Hood-Williams, J. and Harrison, W.C. (1998) ' "It's all in the small print ...": archiving and qualitative research', *BSA Network*, 70: 8–9.

Hough, M. and Mayhew, P. (1983) *The British Crime Survey: First Report*. London: HMSO.

Hough, M. and Mayhew, P. (1985) *Taking Account of Crime*. London: HMSO.

Hunt, J.C. (1989) *Psychoanalytic Aspects of Fieldwork*. University Paper Series on Qualitative Research Methods, Vol. 18. Newbury Park, CA: Sage.

Jefferson, T. (1996a) 'From "little fairy boy" to "the compleat destroyer": subjectivity and transformation in the biography of Mike Tyson', in M. Mac an Ghaill (ed.), *Understanding Masculinities: Social Relations and Cultural Arenas*. London: Routledge. pp. 153–67.

Jefferson, T. (1996b) ' "Tougher than the rest": Mike Tyson and the destructive desires of masculinity', *Arena Journal*, 6: 89–105.

Jefferson, T. (1997) 'The Tyson rape trial: the law, feminism and emotional "truth" ', *Social and Legal Studies*, 6 (2): 281–301.

Jefferson, T. (1998) 'Muscle, "hard men", and "iron" Mike Tyson: reflections on desire, anxiety and the embodiment of masculinity', *Body and Society*, 4 (1): 77–98.

Jones, T., MacLean, B. and Young, J. (1986) *The Islington Crime Survey*. Aldershot: Gower.

Josselson, R. (1992) *The Space between Us: Exploring the Dimensions of Human Relationships*. San Francisco: Jossey Bass.

Josselson, R. (1995) 'Imagining the real: empathy, narrative and the dialogic self', in R. Josselson and A. Lieblich (eds), *The Narrative Study of Lives*, Vol. 3. London: Sage. pp. 27–44.

Junger, M. (1987) 'Women's experiences of sexual harassment', *British Journal of Criminology*, 27 (4): 358–83.

Klein, M. (1988a) *Love, Guilt and Reparation and Other Works, 1921–1945*. London: Virago.

Klein, M. (1988b) *Envy and Gratitude and Other Works, 1946–1963*. London: Virago.

Kroger, J. (1993) 'Identity and context: how the identity statuses choose their match', in R. Josselson and A. Lieblich (eds), *The Narrative Study of Lives*, Vol. 1. London: Sage. pp. 130–62.

Kvale, S. (1999) 'The psychoanalytic interview as qualitative research', *Qualitative Inquiry*, 5 (1): 87–113.

Labov, W. (1972) 'The transformation of experience in narrative syntax', in W. Labov (ed.), *Language in the Inner City*. Philadelphia: University of Pennsylvania Press.

Linde, C. (1993) *Life Stories: the Creation of Coherence*. Oxford: Oxford University Press.

Lindquist, J.H. and Duke, J.M. (1982) 'The elderly victim at risk: explaining the fear-victimization paradox', *Criminology: an Interdisciplinary Journal*, 20 (1): 115–26.

Madill, A., Jordan, A. and Shirley, C. (2000) 'Objectivity and reliability in qualitative analysis: realist, contextualist and radical constructionist epistemologies', *British Journal of Psychology*, 91: 1–20.

Maguire, M. (1982) *Burglary in a Dwelling: the Offence, the Offender and the Victim*. London: Heinemann.

Maynard, M. (1994) 'Introduction', in M. Maynard and J. Purvis (eds), *Researching Women's Lives from a Feminist Perspective*. London: Taylor and Francis. pp. 10–26.

Maynard, M. and Purvis, J. (eds) (1994) *Researching Women's Lives from a Feminist Perspective*. London: Taylor and Francis.

Milgram, S. (1974) *Obedience to Authority*. New York: Harper and Row.

Miller, W.L. and Crabtree, B.F. (1994) 'Clinical research', in N. Denzin and Y. Lincoln (eds), *Handbook of Qualitative Research*. London: Sage. pp. 340–52.

Mirrlees-Black, C., Mayhew, P. and Percy, A. (1996) *The 1996 British Crime Survey: England and Wales*. Home Office Statistical Bulletin, Issue 19/96. Research and Statistics Directorate. London: Home Office.

Mishler, E.G. (1986) *Research Interviewing: Context and Narrative*. Cambridge, MA: Harvard University Press.

Murphy, G. and Kovach, J.K. (1972) *Historical Introduction to Modern Psychology*, 6th edn (first published 1928). London: Routledge and Kegan Paul.

Murray, C. (1990) *The Emerging British Underclass* (with responses by Frank Field, Joan C. Brown, Nicholas Deakin and Alan Walker). London: IEA Health and Welfare Unit.

Oakley, A. (1982) 'Interviewing women: a contradiction in terms?', in H. Roberts (ed.), *Doing Feminist Research*. London: Routledge and Kegan Paul. pp. 30–61.

Ogden, T. (1994) *Subjects of Analysis*. London: Karnac.

Olesen, V. (1994) 'Feminisms and models of qualitative research', in N. Denzin and Y. Lincoln (eds), *Handbook of Qualitative Research*. London: Sage. pp. 158–74.

Pain, R.H. (1993) 'Women's fear of sexual violence: explaining the spatial paradox', in H. Jones (ed.), *Crime and the Urban Environment*. Aldershot: Avebury. pp. 55–68.

Pain, R.H. (1995) 'Elderly women and fear of violent crime: the least likely victims. A reconsideration of the extent and nature of risk', *British Journal of Criminology*, 35 (4): 584–98.

Plummer, K. (1995) *Telling Sexual Stories: Power, Change and Social Worlds*. London: Routledge.

Polkinghorne, D.E. (1988) *Narrative Knowing and the Human Sciences*. Albany: SUNY Press.

Reason, P. and Rowan, J. (1981) *Human Inquiry: a Sourcebook of New Paradigm Research*. Chichester: Wiley.

Richards, T.J. and Richards, L. (1994) 'Using computers in qualitative research', in N. Denzin and Y. Lincoln. *Handbook of Qualitative Research*. London: Sage. pp. 445–62.

Riessman, C.K. (1993) *Narrative Analysis*. Qualitative Research Methods Series, 30. Newbury Park, CA: Sage.

Riger, S., Gordon, M. and Bailley, R. (1978) 'Women's fear of crime: from blaming to restricting the victim', *Victimology*, 3: 274–84.

Riviere, J. (1964) 'Hate, greed and aggression', in M. Klein and J. Riviere (eds), *Love, Hate and Reparation*. London: Norton. pp. 3–53.

Roberts, H. (ed.) (1982) *Doing Feminist Research*. London: Routledge and Kegan Paul.

Roper, M. (1996) 'Seduction and succession: circuits of homosocial desire in management', in D. Collinson and J. Hearn (eds), *Men as Managers, Managers as Men*. London: Sage. pp. 210–26.

Rosenthal, G. (1990) 'The structure and "Gestalt" of autobiographies and its methodological consequences', unpublished paper presented to the Twelfth World Congress of Sociology, Madrid.

Rosenthal, G. (1993) 'Reconstruction of life stories: principles of selection in generating stories for narrative biographical interviews', in R. Josselson and A. Lieblich (eds), *The Narrative Study of Lives*, Vol. 1. London: Sage. pp. 59–91.

Rosenthal, G. and Bar-On, D. (1992) 'A biographical case study of a victimizer's daughter', *Journal of Narrative and Life History*, 2 (2): 105–27.

Sandler, J., Dare, C. and Holder, A. (1990) *The Patient and the Analyst*, 2nd edn (first published 1973). London: Maresfield.

Scharff, D. (1992) *Refinding the Object and Reclaiming the Self*. Northvale, NJ and London: Jason Aronson.

Scheurich, J.J. (1997) *Research Method in the Postmodern*. London: Falmer.

Schutze, F. (1992) 'Pressure and guilt: the experience of a young German soldier in World War Two and its biographical implications', *International Sociology*, 7 (2): 187–208; 7 (3): 347–67.

Scott, A. (1996) *Real Events Revisited*. London: Virago.

Sereny, G. (1995) *The Case of Mary Bell: a Portrait of a Child who Murdered*, 2nd edn (first published 1972). London: Pimlico.

Sereny, G. (1998) *Cries Unheard: the Story of Mary Bell*. London: Macmillan.

Sparks, R. (1992) 'Reason and unreason in "left realism": some problems in the constitution of fear of crime', in R. Matthews and J. Young (eds), *Issues in Realist Criminology*. London: Sage. pp. 119–35.

Stanko, E.A. (1985) *Intimate Intrusions*. London: Unwin Hyman.

Stanko, E.A. (1990) *Everyday Violence: How Men and Women Experience Sexual and Physical Danger*. London: Pandora.

Stanko, E.A. and Hobdell, K. (1993) 'Assault on men: masculinity and male victimization', *British Journal of Criminology*, 33 (3): 400–15.

Stanley, L. and Wise, S. (1983) *Breaking Out: Feminist Consciousness and Feminist Research*. London: Routledge and Kegan Paul.

Symington, J. and Symington, N. (1996) *The Clinical Thinking of Wilfred Bion*. London: Routledge.

Walkerdine, V. (1997) *Daddy's Girl*. London: Macmillan.

Walsh, D. (1980) *Break-ins: Burglary from Private Houses*. London: Constable.

Watkins, J.M. (1994–5) 'A postmodern critical theory of research use', *Knowledge and Policy*, 7: 55–77.

Willis, P. (1977) *Learning to Labour*. Farnborough, UK: Saxon House.

Wilson, E.A. (1997) *Neural Geographies*. London: Routledge.

Woodward, C. (1996) 'Hearing voices? Methodological, epistemological and practical issues in research when telling participants' stories of childhood sexual abuse', paper presented at the International Conference of Social Science Methods, Essex, UK, July.

Wright, R.T. and Decker, S. (1994) *Burglars on the Job: Streetlife and Residential Break-ins*. Boston: Northeastern University Press.

INDEX